# ANTONY AND CLEOPATRA

*William Shakespeare*

D0104812

TECHNICAL DIRECTOR Maxwell Krohn
EDITORIAL DIRECTOR Justin Kestler
MANAGING EDITOR Ben Florman

SERIES EDITORS Boomie Aglietti, Justin Kestler
PRODUCTION Christian Lorentzen

WRITERS Ross Douthat, David Hopson
EDITORS John Crowther, Benjamin Morgan

Copyright © 2002 by SparkNotes LLC

All rights reserved. No part of this book may be used or reproduced in any manner
whatsoever without the written permission of the Publisher.

SPARKNOTES is a registered trademark of SparkNotes LLC.

This edition published by Spark Publishing

Spark Publishing
A Division of SparkNotes LLC
120 Fifth Avenue, 8th Floor
New York, NY 10011

Any book purchased without a cover is stolen property, reported as "unsold and
destroyed" to the Publisher, who receives no payment for such "stripped books."

02 03 04 05 SN 9 8 7 6 5 4 3 2 1

Please send all comments and questions or report errors to
feedback@sparknotes.com.

Library of Congress information available upon request

Printed and bound in the United States

RRD-C

ISBN 1-58663-471-2

# INTRODUCTION: A PROLOGUE FROM THE BARD

Brave scholars, blessed with time and energy,
  At school, fair Harvard, set about to glean,
From dusty tomes and modern poetry,
  All truths and knowledge formerly unseen.
From forth the hungry minds of these good folk
  Study guides, star-floss'd, soon came to life;
Whose deep and deft analysis awoke
  The latent "A"s of those in lit'rary strife.
Aim far past passing—insight from our trove
  Will free your comprehension from its cage.
Our SparkNotes' worth, online we also prove;
  Behold this book! Same brains, but paper page.
If patient or "whatever," please attend,
  What you have missed, our toil shall strive to mend.

# Contents

NOTE: This SparkNote refers to the text of *Antony and Cleopatra* given in *The Norton Shakespeare*, edited by Stephen Greenblatt. Other editions of the play may differ in line numbering, spelling, punctuation, and diction.

# Context

THE MOST INFLUENTIAL WRITER in all of English literature, William Shakespeare was born in 1564 to a successful middle-class glove maker in Stratford-upon-Avon, England. Shakespeare attended grammar school, but his formal education proceeded no further. In 1582 he married an older woman, Anne Hathaway, and had three children with her. Around 1590 he left his family behind and traveled to London to work as an actor and playwright. Public and critical acclaim quickly followed, and Shakespeare eventually became the most popular playwright in England and part-owner of the Globe Theater. His career bridged the reigns of Elizabeth I (ruled 1558–1603) and James I (ruled 1603–1625), and he was a favorite of both monarchs. Indeed, James granted Shakespeare's company the greatest possible compliment by bestowing upon its members the title of King's Men. Wealthy and renowned, Shakespeare retired to Stratford and died in 1616 at the age of fifty-two. At the time of Shakespeare's death, literary luminaries such as Ben Jonson hailed his works as timeless.

Shakespeare's works were collected and printed in various editions in the century following his death, and by the early eighteenth century his reputation as the greatest poet ever to write in English was well established. The unprecedented admiration garnered by his works led to a fierce curiosity about Shakespeare's life, but the dearth of biographical information has left many details of Shakespeare's personal history shrouded in mystery. Some people have concluded from this fact and from Shakespeare's modest education that Shakespeare's plays were actually written by someone else—Francis Bacon and the Earl of Oxford are the two most popular candidates—but the support for this claim is overwhelmingly circumstantial, and the theory is not taken seriously by many scholars.

In the absence of credible evidence to the contrary, Shakespeare must be viewed as the author of the thirty-seven plays and 154 sonnets that bear his name. The legacy of this body of work is immense. A number of Shakespeare's plays seem to have transcended even the category of brilliance, becoming so influential as to affect profoundly the course of Western literature and culture ever after.

Scholars believe that Shakespeare wrote *Antony and Cleopatra* in 1606, immediately after *Macbeth,* and it is one of the last great tragedies that Shakespeare produced. The most geographically sweeping of Shakespeare's plays, *Antony and Cleopatra*'s setting is the entire Roman Empire, its backdrop the well-documented history of Octavius Caesar, Marc Antony, and Cleopatra. Shakespeare's primary source for *Antony and Cleopatra* was the *Life* of Marcus Antonius contained in Plutarch's *Lives of the Noble Grecians and Romans,* which was translated into English by Sir Thomas North in 1579. North's language was so rich that Shakespeare incorporated large, relatively unchanged excerpts of it into his text. The plot of the play also remains close to North's history, although characters like Enobarbus and Cleopatra's attendants are largely Shakespearean creations.

The action of the story takes place roughly two years after the events of Shakespeare's earlier play about the Roman Empire, *Julius Caesar.* At the beginning of that tragedy, Caesar has triumphed over his rival Pompey the Great, the father of young Pompey in *Antony and Cleopatra,* and aspires to kingship. Caesar is then assassinated by Cassius and Brutus, who hope to preserve the Roman Republic. Instead, Cassius and Brutus are defeated by Mark Antony and Octavius Caesar, Julius's nephew, who then join Marcus Aemilius Lepidus to create a three-man government, or triumvirate, over the empire.

Historically, the action of *Antony and Cleopatra* takes place over a ten-year span, whereas in the play the story is compressed to fit the needs of the stage. Antony is clearly much older than he was in *Julius Caesar,* and his political instincts seem to be waning. Octavius Caesar was only a minor character in the earlier play, but here he comes into his own as the man who will rise to become the first Roman emperor. Most of the political battles and machinations depicted are historically accurate, as is the romance of the title characters.

# PLOT OVERVIEW

**M**ARK ANTONY, ONE OF THE THREE RULERS of the Roman Empire, spends his time in Egypt, living a life of decadence and conducting an affair with the country's beautiful queen, Cleopatra. When a message arrives informing him that his wife, Fulvia, is dead and that Pompey is raising an army to rebel against the triumvirate, Antony decides to return to Rome. In Antony's absence, Octavius Caesar and Lepidus, his fellow triumvirs, worry about Pompey's increasing strength. Caesar condemns Antony for neglecting his duties as a statesman and military officer in order to live a decadent life by Cleopatra's side.

The news of his wife's death and imminent battle pricks Antony's sense of duty, and he feels compelled to return to Rome. Upon his arrival, he and Caesar quarrel, while Lepidus ineffectually tries to make peace. Realizing that an alliance is necessary to defeat Pompey, Antony and Caesar agree that Antony will marry Caesar's sister, Octavia, who will solidify their loyalty to one another. Enobarbus, Antony's closest friend, predicts to Caesar's men that, despite the marriage, Antony will surely return to Cleopatra.

In Egypt, Cleopatra learns of Antony's marriage and flies into a jealous rage. However, when a messenger delivers word that Octavia is plain and unimpressive, Cleopatra becomes confident that she will win Antony back. The triumvirs meet Pompey and settle their differences without going to battle. Pompey agrees to keep peace in exchange for rule over Sicily and Sardinia. That evening, the four men drink to celebrate their truce. One of Pompey's soldiers discloses to him a plan to assassinate the triumvirs, thereby delivering world power into Pompey's hands, but Pompey dismisses the scheme as an affront to his honor. Meanwhile, one of Antony's generals wins a victory over the kingdom of Parthia.

Antony and Octavia depart for Athens. Once they are gone, Caesar breaks his truce, wages war against Pompey, and defeats him. After using Lepidus's army to secure a victory, he accuses Lepidus of treason, imprisons him, and confiscates his land and possessions. This news angers Antony, as do the rumors that Caesar has been speaking out against him in public. Octavia pleads with Antony to maintain a peaceful relationship with her brother. Should Antony

3

and Caesar fight, she says, her affections would be painfully divided. Antony dispatches her to Rome on a peace mission, and quickly returns to Egypt and Cleopatra. There, he raises a large army to fight Caesar, and Caesar, incensed over Antony's treatment of his sister, responds in kind. Caesar commands his army and navy to Egypt. Ignoring all advice to the contrary, Antony elects to fight him at sea, allowing Cleopatra to command a ship despite Enobarbus's strong objections. Antony's forces lose the battle when Cleopatra's ship flees and Antony's follows, leaving the rest of the fleet vulnerable to attack.

Antony despairs, condemning Cleopatra for leading him into infamy but quickly forgiving her. He and Cleopatra send requests to their conqueror: Antony asks to be allowed to live in Egypt, while Cleopatra asks that her kingdom be passed down to her rightful heirs. Caesar dismisses Antony's request, but he promises Cleopatra a fair hearing if she betrays her lover. Cleopatra seems to be giving thought to Caesar's message when Antony barges in, curses her for her treachery, and orders the innocent messenger whipped. When, moments later, Antony forgives Cleopatra, Enobarbus decides that his master is finished and defects to Caesar's camp.

Antony meets Caesar's troops in battle and scores an unexpected victory. When he learns of Enobarbus's desertion, Antony laments his own bad fortune, which he believes has corrupted an honorable man. He sends his friend's possessions to Caesar's camp and returns to Cleopatra to celebrate his victory. Enobarbus, undone by shame at his own disloyalty, bows under the weight of his guilt and dies. Another day brings another battle, and once again Antony meets Caesar at sea. As before, the Egyptian fleet proves treacherous; it abandons the fight and leaves Antony to suffer defeat. Convinced that his lover has betrayed him, Antony vows to kill Cleopatra. In order to protect herself, she quarters herself in her monument and sends word that she has committed suicide. Antony, racked with grief, determines to join his queen in the afterlife. He commands one of his attendants to fulfill his promise of unquestioned service and kill him. The attendant kills himself instead. Antony then falls on his own sword, but the wound is not immediately fatal. He is carried to Cleopatra's monument, where the lovers are reunited briefly before Antony's death. Caesar takes the queen prisoner, planning to display her in Rome as a testament to the might of his empire, but she learns of his plan and kills herself with the help of several poisonous snakes. Caesar has her buried beside Antony.

# CHARACTER LIST

*Antony*   A once fierce and feared soldier who rules the Roman
Empire along with Octavius Caesar and Lepidus.
When the play opens, Antony has neglected his duties
as a ruler in order to live in Egypt, where he carries on a
highly visible love affair with Cleopatra. His loyalty is
divided between the Western and Eastern worlds; he is
torn between the sense of duty and the desire to seek
pleasure, between reason and passion. While he feels
the need to reaffirm the honor that has made him a
celebrated Roman hero, he is also madly in love
with Cleopatra.

*Cleopatra* The queen of Egypt and Antony's lover. A highly
attractive woman who once seduced Julius Caesar,
Cleopatra delights in the thought that she has caught
Antony like a fish. In matters of love, as in all things,
Cleopatra favors high drama: her emotions are as
volatile as they are theatrical, and, regardless of
whether her audience is her handmaid or the emperor
of Rome, she always offers a top-notch performance.
Although she tends to make a spectacle of her
emotions, one cannot doubt the genuine nature of her
love for Antony. Shakespeare makes clear that the
queen *does* love the general, even if her loyalty is
sometimes misplaced.

*Octavius Caesar* The nephew and adopted son of Julius Caesar.
Octavius rules the Roman Empire with Antony and
Lepidus. Relations between Caesar and Antony are
strained throughout the play, for the young triumvir
believes that Antony squanders his time and neglects
his duties while in Egypt. Ambitious and extremely
pragmatic, Octavius lacks Antony's military might as a
general, but his careful and stoic reasoning enables him
to avoid Antony's tendency toward heroic or romantic

CHARACTER LIST

folly. Destined to be the first Roman emperor (later renamed Caesar Augustus), he symbolizes "Western" values in the play, which stand opposed to the exotic lures of Cleopatra's "East."

*Enobarbus* Antony's most loyal supporter. Worldly and cynical, Enobarbus is friendly with the subordinates of both Pompey and Caesar, yet stays faithful to his master even after Antony makes grave political and military missteps. He abandons Antony only when the general appears to be completely finished.

*Marcus Aemilius Lepidus* The third member of the triumvirate and the weakest, both politically and personally. Lepidus's rather desperate attempts to keep the peace between Caesar and Antony fail when Caesar imprisons him after the defeat of Pompey.

*Pompey* The son of a great general who was one of Julius Caesar's partners in power. Pompey is young and popular with the Roman people, and he possesses enough military might to stand as a legitimate threat to the triumvirs. He fancies himself honorable for refusing to allow one of his men to kill the unsuspecting Caesar, Antony, and Lepidus when they are his guests.

*Octavia* Octavius Caesar's sister. Octavia marries Antony in order to cement an alliance between the two triumvirs. She is a victim of Antony's deception, and her meekness, purity, and submission make her the paradigm of Roman womanhood, and Cleopatra's polar opposite.

*Charmian and Iras* Cleopatra's faithful attendants.

*The Soothsayer* An Egyptian fortune-teller who follows Antony to Rome and predicts that his fortune will always pale in comparison to Caesar's.

*Dolabella* One of Octavius Caesar's men. Dolabella is assigned to guard the captive Cleopatra.

*Agrippa*   One of Octavius Caesar's officers. Agrippa leads the retreat from Antony's unexpectedly powerful forces.

*Camidius*   A general in Antony's army. After the battle in which Antony follows Cleopatra's lead and flees, Camidius surrenders and defects to Caesar's side.

*Ventidius*   A Roman soldier under Antony's command. Ventidius leads the legions to victory against the kingdom of Parthia. Although a competent fighter, he cautiously decides not to push his troops further into battle, for fear that winning too much glory would sour his relationship with Antony.

*Scarus*   A brave young soldier serving under Antony. Scarus garners fantastic wounds in the battle against Caesar's army, and begs for the opportunity to win more.

*Proculeius*   One of Caesar's soldiers, who proves untrustworthy.

*Diomedes*   Cleopatra's servant. She employs Diomedes to bring to Antony the message that she has not committed suicide but is still alive.

*Eros*   An attendant serving Antony. Eros's love for his master compels him to refuse Antony's order that Eros kill him.

*Menas*   An ambitious young soldier under Pompey. During the dinner party that Pompey hosts for the triumvirate, Menas asks for permission to kill Caesar, Antony, and Lepidus, which would result in the control of the world falling into his master's hands.

*Seleucus*   Cleopatra's treasurer, who betrays his master.

*Clown*   An Egyptian who brings a basket of figs containing poisonous snakes to Cleopatra.

*Decretas*   One of Antony's soldiers.

# ANALYSIS OF MAJOR CHARACTERS

## MARK ANTONY

Throughout the play, Antony grapples with the conflict between his love for Cleopatra and his duties to the Roman Empire. In Act I, scene i, he engages Cleopatra in a conversation about the nature and depth of their love, dismissing the duties he has neglected for her sake: "Let Rome in Tiber melt, and the wide arch / Of the ranged empire fall" (I.i.35–36). In the very next scene, however, Antony worries that he is about to "lose [him]self in dotage" (I.ii.106) and fears that the death of his wife is only one of the ills that his "idleness doth hatch" (I.ii.119). Thus, Antony finds himself torn between the Rome of his duty and the Alexandria of his pleasure. The geographical poles that draw him in opposite directions represent deep-seated conflicts between his reason and emotion, his sense of duty and his desire, his obligations to the state and his private needs.

Antony's understanding of himself, however, cannot bear the stress of such tension. In his mind, he is first and foremost a Roman hero of the first caliber. He won his position as one of the three leaders of the world by vanquishing the treacherous Brutus and Cassius, who conspired to assassinate his predecessor, Julius Caesar. He often recalls the golden days of his own heroism, but now that he is entangled in an affair with the Egyptian queen, his memories do little more than demonstrate how far he has strayed from his ideal self. As he points out to Octavia in Act III, scene iv, his current actions imperil his honor, and without his honor—the defining characteristic of the Roman hero—he can no longer be Antony: "If I lose my honor, / I lose myself. Better I were not yours / Than yours so branchless" (III.iv.22–24). Later, having suffered defeat at the hands of both Caesar and Cleopatra, Antony returns to the imagery of the stripped tree as he laments, "[T]his pine is barked / That overtopped them all" (IV.xiii.23–24). Rather than amend his identity to accommodate these defeats, Antony chooses to take his own life, an act that restores him to his brave and indomitable former self. In suicide, Antony manages to convince himself and the world (as represented by Cleopatra and Caesar) that he is "a Roman by a Roman / Valiantly vanquished" (IV.xvi.59–60).

## CLEOPATRA

The assortment of perspectives from which we see Cleopatra illustrates the varying understandings of her as a decadent foreign woman and a noble ruler. As Philo and Demetrius take the stage in Act I, scene i, their complaints about Antony's neglected duties frame the audience's understanding of Cleopatra, the queen for whom Antony risks his reputation. Within the first ten lines of the play, the men declare Cleopatra a lustful "gipsy," a description that is repeated throughout the play as though by a chorus (I.i.10). Cleopatra is labeled a "wrangling queen" (I.i.50), a "slave" (I.iv.19), an "Egyptian dish" (II.vi.123), and a "whore" (III.vi.67); she is called "Salt Cleopatra" (II.i.21) and an enchantress who has made Antony "the noble ruin of her magic" (III.x.18).

But to view Cleopatra as such is to reduce her character to the rather narrow perspective of the Romans, who, standing to lose their honor or kingdoms through her agency, are most threatened by her. Certainly this threat has much to do with Cleopatra's beauty and open sexuality, which, as Enobarbus points out in his famous description of her in Act II, scene ii, is awe-inspiring. But it is also a performance. Indeed, when Cleopatra takes the stage, she does so as an actress, elevating her passion, grief, and outrage to the most dramatic and captivating level. As Enobarbus says, the queen did not walk through the street, but rather

> Hop[ped] forty paces . . .
> And having lost her breath, she spoke and panted,
> That she did make defect perfection,
> And breathless, pour breath forth.
> (II.ii.235–238)

Whether whispering sweet words of love to Antony or railing at a supposedly disloyal servant, Cleopatra leaves her onlookers breathless. As Antony notes, she is a woman "[w]hom everything becomes—to chide, to laugh / To weep" (I.i.51–52). It is this ability to be the perfect embodiment of all things—beauty and ugliness, virtue and vice—that Cleopatra stands to lose after her defeat by Caesar. By parading her through the streets of Rome as his trophy, he intends to reduce her character to a single, base element—to immortalize her as a whore. If Antony cannot allow his conception of self to expand to incorporate his defeats, then Cleopatra cannot allow hers to be stripped to the image of a boy actor "squeaking Cleopatra . . . / I'th' posture of a whore" (V.ii.216–217). Cleopatra often behaves childishly and with relentless self-absorption; nevertheless, her charisma, strength, and indomitable will make her one of Shakespeare's strongest, most awe-inspiring female characters.

## OCTAVIUS CAESAR

Ocatavius Caesar is both a menacing adversary for Antony and a rigid representation of Roman law and order. He is not a two-dimensional villain, though, since his frustrations with the ever-neglectful Antony seem justified. When he complains to Lepidus that he resents having to "bear / So great weight in [Antony's] lightness," we certainly understand his concern (I.iv.24–25). He does not emerge as a particularly likable character—his treatment of Lepidus, for instance, betrays the cruel underside of Caesar's aggressive ambitions—but he is a complicated one. He is, in other words, convincingly human. There is, perhaps, no better example of Caesar's humanity than his conflicted feelings about Antony. For a good deal of the play, Caesar seems bent, rather ruthlessly, on destroying Antony. When he achieves this desired end, however, he does not relish the moment as we might expect. Instead, he mourns the loss of a great soldier and musters enough compassion to be not only fair-minded but also fair-hearted, commanding that the lovers be buried beside one another.

CHARACTER ANALYSIS

# THEMES, MOTIFS & SYMBOLS

## THEMES

*Themes are the fundamental and often universal ideas explored in a literary work.*

### THE STRUGGLE BETWEEN REASON AND EMOTION

In his opening lines to Demetrius, Philo complains that Antony has abandoned the military endeavors on which his reputation is based for Cleopatra's sake. His criticism of Antony's "dotage," or stupidity, introduces a tension between reason and emotion that runs throughout the play (I.i.1). Antony and Cleopatra's first exchange heightens this tension, as they argue whether their love can be put into words and understood or whether it exceeds such faculties and boundaries of reason. If, according to Roman consensus, Antony is the military hero and disciplined statesmen that Caesar and others believe him to be, then he seems to have happily abandoned his reason in order to pursue his passion. He declares: "Let Rome in Tiber melt, and the wide arch / Of the ranged empire fall" (I.i.35–36). The play, however, is more concerned with the battle between reason and emotion than the triumph of one over the other, and this battle is waged most forcefully in the character of Antony. More than any other character in the play, Antony vacillates between Western and Eastern sensibilities, feeling pulled by both his duty to the empire and his desire for pleasure, his want of military glory and his passion for Cleopatra. Soon after his nonchalant dismissal of Caesar's messenger, the empire, and his duty to it, he chastises himself for his neglect and commits to return to Rome, lest he "lose [him]self in dotage" (I.ii.106).

As the play progresses, Antony continues to inhabit conflicting identities that play out the struggle between reason and emotion. At one moment, he is the vengeful war hero whom Caesar praises and fears. Soon thereafter, he sacrifices his military position by unwisely allowing Cleopatra to determine his course of action. As his Roman allies—even the ever-faithful Enobarbus—abandon him, Antony feels that he has, indeed, lost himself in dotage, and he determines to rescue his noble identity by taking his own life. At first, this course of action may appear to be a triumph of reason over passion, of Western sensibilities over Eastern ones, but the play is not that simple. Although Antony dies believing himself a man of honor, discipline, and reason, our understanding of him is not nearly as straightforward. In order to come to terms with Antony's character, we must analyze the aspects of his identity that he ignores. He is, in the end, a man ruled by passion as much as by reason. Likewise, the play offers us a worldview in which one sensibility cannot easily dominate another. Reason cannot ever fully conquer the passions, nor can passion wholly undo reason.

## THE CLASH OF EAST AND WEST

Although *Antony and Cleopatra* details the conflict between Rome and Egypt, giving us an idea of the Elizabethan perceptions of the difference between Western and Eastern cultures, it does not make a definitive statement about which culture ultimately triumphs. In the play, the Western and Eastern poles of the world are characterized by those who inhabit them: Caesar, for instance, embodies the stoic duty of the West, while Cleopatra, in all her theatrical grandeur, represents the free-flowing passions of the East. Caesar's concerns throughout the play are certainly imperial: he means to invade foreign lands in order to invest them with traditions and sensibilities of his own. But the play resists siding with this imperialist impulse. Shakespeare, in other words, does not align the play's sympathies with the West; *Antony and Cleopatra* can hardly be read as propaganda for Western domination. On the contrary, the Roman understanding of Cleopatra and her kingdom seems exceedingly superficial. To Caesar, the queen of Egypt is little more than a whore with a flair for drama. His perspective allows little room for the real power of Cleopatra's sexuality—she can, after all, persuade the most decorated of generals to follow her into ignoble retreat. Similarly, it allows little room for the indomitable strength of her will, which she demonstrates so forcefully at the end of the play as she refuses to allow herself to be turned into a "Egyptian puppet" for the entertainment of the Roman masses (V.ii.204).

In *Antony and Cleopatra,* West meets East, but it does not, regardless of Caesar's triumph over the land of Egypt, conquer it. Cleopatra's suicide suggests that something of the East's spirit, the freedoms and passions that are not represented in the play's conception of the West, cannot be subsumed by Caesar's victory. The play suggests that the East will live on as a visible and unconquerable counterpoint to the West, bound as inseparably and eternally as Antony and Cleopatra are in their tomb.

## THE DEFINITION OF HONOR

Throughout the play, characters define honor variously, and often in ways that are not intuitive. As Antony prepares to meet Caesar in battle, he determines that he "will live / Or bathe [his] dying honour in the blood / Shall make it live again" (IV.ii.5–7). Here, he explicitly links the notion of honor to to that of death, suggesting the latter as a surefire means of achieving the former. The play bears out this assertion, since, although Antony and Cleopatra kill themselves for different reasons, they both imagine that the act invests them with honor. In death, Antony returns to his identity as a true, noble Roman, becoming "a Roman by a Roman / Valiantly vanquished" (IV.xvi.59–60), while Cleopatra resolves to "bury him, and then what's brave, what's noble, / Let's do it after the high Roman fashion" (IV.xvi.89–90). At first, the queen's words seem to suggest that honor is a distinctly Roman attribute, but Cleopatra's death, which is her means of ensuring that she remains her truest, most uncompromised self, is distinctly against Rome. In *Antony and Cleopatra,* honor seems less a function of Western or Eastern culture than of the characters' determination to define themselves on their own terms. Both Antony and Cleopatra secure honorable deaths by refusing to compromise their identities.

THEMES

## MOTIFS

*Motifs are recurring structures, contrasts, or literary devices that can help to develop and inform the text's major themes.*

### EXTRAVAGANT DECLARATIONS OF LOVE

In Act I, scene i, Antony and Cleopatra argue over whether their love for one another can be measured and articulated:

CLEOPATRA: [to Antony] If it be love indeed, tell me how much.
　ANTONY:　There's beggary in the love that can be reckoned.
CLEOPATRA: I'll set a bourn how far to be beloved.
　　ANTONY:　Then must thou needs find out new heaven, new
　　　　　　earth.

(I.i.14–17)

This exchange sets the tone for the way that love will be discussed and understood throughout the play. Cleopatra expresses the expectation that love should be declared or demonstrated grandly. She wants to hear and see exactly how much Antony loves her. Love, in *Antony and Cleopatra,* is not comprised of private intimacies, as it is in *Romeo and Juliet.* Instead, love belongs to the public arena. In the lines quoted above, Cleopatra claims that she will set the boundaries of her lover's affections, and Antony responds that, to do so, she will need to discover uncharted territories. By likening their love to the discovery and claim of "new heaven, new earth," the couple links private emotions to affairs of state. Love, in other words, becomes an extension of politics, with the annexation of another's heart analogous to the conquering of a foreign land.

### PUBLIC DISPLAYS OF AFFECTION

In *Antony and Cleopatra,* public displays of affection are generally understood to be expressions of political power and allegiance. Caesar, for example, laments that Octavia arrives in Rome without the fanfare of a proper entourage because it betrays her weakness: without an accompanying army of horses, guardsmen, and trumpeters, she cannot possibly be recognized as Caesar's sister or Antony's wife. The connection between public display and power is one that the characters—especially Caesar and Cleopatra—understand well. After Antony's death, their battle of wills revolves around Caesar's desire to exhibit the Egyptian queen on the streets of Rome as a sign of his triumph. Cleopatra refuses such an end, choosing instead to take her own life. Even this act is meant as a public performance, however: decked in her grandest royal robes and playing the part of the tragic lover, Cleopatra intends her last act to be as much a defiance of Caesar's power as a gesture of romantic devotion. For death, she claims, is "the way / To fool their preparation and to conquer / Their most absurd intents" (V.ii.220–222).

### FEMALE SEXUALITY
Throughout the play, the male characters rail against the power of female sexuality. Caesar and his men condemn Antony for the weakness that makes him bow to the Egyptian queen, but they clearly lay the blame for his downfall on Cleopatra. On the rare occasion that the Romans do not refer to her as a whore, they describe her as an enchantress whose beauty casts a dangerous spell over men. As Enobarbus notes, Cleopatra possesses the power to warp the minds and judgment of all men, even "holy priests" who "[b]less her" when she acts like a whore (II.ii.244–245).

The unapologetic openness of Cleopatra's sexuality stands to threaten the Romans. But they are equally obsessed with the powers of Octavia's sexuality. Caesar's sister, who, in beauty and temperament stands as Cleopatra's opposite, is nevertheless considered to possess power enough to mend the triumvir's damaged relationship: Caesar and Antony expect that she will serve to "knit [their] hearts / With an unslipping knot" (II.ii.132–133). In this way, women are saddled with both the responsibility for men's political alliances and the blame for their personal failures.

## SYMBOLS

*Symbols are objects, characters, figures, or colors used to represent abstract ideas or concepts.*

### SHAPE-CHANGING CLOUDS
In Act IV, scene xv, Antony likens his shifting sense of self to a cloud that changes shape as it tumbles across the sky. Just as the cloud turns from "a bear or lion, / A towered citadel, a pendent rock," Antony seems to change from the reputed conqueror into a debased victim (IV.xv.3–4). As he says to Eros, his uncharacteristic defeat, both on the battlefield and in matters of love, makes it difficult for him to "hold this visible shape" (IV.xv.14).

S Y M B O L S

## Cleopatra's Fleeing Ships

The image of Cleopatra's fleeing ships is presented twice in the play. Antony twice does battle with Caesar at sea, and both times his navy is betrayed by the queen's retreat. The ships remind us of Cleopatra's inconstancy and of the inconstancy of human character in the play. One cannot be sure of Cleopatra's allegiance: it is uncertain whether she flees out of fear or because she realizes it would be politically savvy to align herself with Caesar. Her fleeing ships are an effective symbol of her wavering and changeability.

## The Asps

One of the most memorable symbols in the play comes in its final moments, as Cleopatra applies deadly snakes to her skin. The asps are a prop in the queen's final and most magnificent performance. As she lifts one snake, then another to her breast, they become her children and she a common wet nurse: "Dost thou not see my baby at my breast, / That sucks the nurse asleep?" (V.ii.300–301). The domestic nature of the image contributes to Cleopatra's final metamorphosis, in death, into Antony's wife. She assures him, "Husband, I come" (V.ii.278).

SYMBOLS

# SUMMARY & ANALYSIS

## ACT I, SCENES I–III

### SUMMARY: ACT I, SCENE I

In Egypt, Philo and Demetrius, two Roman soldiers, discuss how their general, Mark Antony, has fallen in love with the Egyptian queen, Cleopatra, and has lost interest in his proper role as one of the three leaders (or triumvirs) of the Roman Empire. Cleopatra and Antony enter, the queen imploring Antony to describe just how much he loves her, when a messenger from Rome greets them. Antony says that he has little interest in hearing Roman news, but Cleopatra tells him that he must listen. She teases Antony for possibly turning away a command from young Octavius Caesar or a rebuke from Antony's wife, Fulvia. When she urges him to return to Rome, Antony claims that Rome means nothing to him. He says that his duty requires him to stay in Alexandria and love Cleopatra. Although the queen doubts the sincerity of his sentiment, her suggestions that Antony hear the news from Rome go unheeded, and the couple exits together. After the lovers have gone, Philo and Demetrius express shock and despair at their general's disrespect for Caesar and the concerns of the empire.

### SUMMARY: ACT I, SCENE II

Cleopatra's attendants ask a soothsayer, or fortune-teller, to reveal their futures. The Soothsayer tells Charmian and Iras, the queen's maids, that their fortunes are the same: their pasts will prove better than their futures, and they shall outlive the queen whom they serve. Cleopatra joins them, complaining that Antony has suddenly turned his mind toward Rome again. She sends Antony's follower Enobarbus to fetch his master, but changes her mind, and as Antony approaches, she leaves to avoid seeing him. A messenger reports to Antony that Fulvia and Lucius, Antony's brother, have mounted an army against Caesar but have lost their battle. When the messenger hesitantly suggests that this event would not have happened had Antony been in Rome, Antony invites the man to speak openly, to "taunt [his] faults / With such full licence as both truth and malice /

Have power to utter" (I.ii.96–98). Another messenger arrives to report that Fulvia is dead. Antony comments that he long desired his wife's death but now wishes her alive again.

Enobarbus arrives and tries to comfort Antony with the thought that Fulvia's death was an event that should be welcomed rather than mourned. Worried that his idleness and devotion to Cleopatra are responsible for these events, as well as a battle being waged by Sextus Pompeius, who is currently attempting to take control of the seas from the triumvirs, Antony decides to break away from Cleopatra and return to Rome.

### SUMMARY: ACT I, SCENE III

Cleopatra orders her servant Alexas to fetch Antony. When Antony enters, Cleopatra feigns a fainting spell, lamenting that Fulvia ever gave Antony leave to come to Egypt. She asks how she can have believed the vows of a man so willing to break his vows to his wife. Antony tells her of the volatile political situation in Rome and of Fulvia's death. Cleopatra notes how little he mourns and predicts that he will grieve as little after her own death. They argue about the depth and truth of his feelings, until Antony finally departs, promising that distance will not threaten their love.

---

### ANALYSIS: ACT I, SCENES I–III

Shakespeare organizes the plot of *Antony and Cleopatra* around the conflict between East and West, Egypt and Rome. He immediately establishes this opposition in the opening scene, when two Roman soldiers pass judgment on their commander, Mark Antony, for surrendering his martial duties to the exotic pleasures of Cleopatra's Egypt. The battle is not merely between two geographically distinct empires but also between two diametrically opposed worldviews. As Philo and Demetrius lament Antony's decline, claiming that his "captain's heart" now serves as "the bellows and the fan / To cool a gipsy's lust," they illustrate a divide between a world that is governed by reason, discipline, and prudence, and another ruled by passion, pleasure, and love (I.i.6–10).

Cleopatra, however, is much more than the high-class prostitute that the Romans believe her to be. Often considered Shakespeare's strongest female character, Cleopatra is a consummate actress. As her first scene with Antony shows, she conducts her affair with the Roman general in a highly theatrical fashion, her actions fueled as

SUMMARY & ANALYSIS

much by the need to create a public spectacle as by the desire to satisfy a private passion. Later, upon learning of Antony's plan to return to Rome, the queen shifts from grief to anger with astonishing speed. No sooner does she recover from a fainting spell than she rails at Antony for his inability to mourn his dead wife adequately. As he prepares to leave, Cleopatra says, "But sir, forgive me, / Since my becomings kill me when they do not / Eye well to you" (I.iii.96-98). Here, "becomings" refers not only to the graces that become or suit the queen but also to her fluid transformations, her many moods, and the many different versions of herself she presents. In Act I, scene i, Antony points to this mutability when he notes that Cleopatra is a woman "[w]hom everything becomes—to chide, to laugh, / To weep" (I.i.51-52). This talent for perpetual change lends Cleopatra her characteristic sense of drama as well as her complexity.

Antony, meanwhile, seems to enjoy indulging in hyperbole as much as Cleopatra. When she tells him that his duties call him home, he declares:

> Let Rome in Tiber melt, and the wide arch
> Of the ranged empire fall. Here is my space.
> Kingdoms are clay. Our dungy earth alike
> Feeds beast as man.
>
> (I.i.35–36)

His speech stands in contrast to the measured, unadorned speech of Philo and Demetrius and, later, Octavius Caesar. Antony delights in depicting himself in heroic terms—indeed, he occupies himself with thoughts of winning nobleness and honor—but already we detect the sharp tension between his rhetoric and his action.

From the beginning of the play, Antony is strongly attracted to both Rome and Egypt, and his loyalty vacillates from one to the other. In these first scenes, he goes from letting "Rome in Tiber melt" to deciding that he "must from this enchanting queen break off" (I.ii.117). His infatuation with the queen is not strong enough to overcome his sense of responsibility to Rome, and while Octavius Caesar, his efficient antagonist, has yet to appear onstage, the lengthy discussion of the strife between Fulvia, Caesar, and young Pompey reminds us of the political context of this love affair. Antony governs a third of the Roman Empire, which has endured decades of civil strife, and he and Caesar, though allies, are not true friends. Such an unstable situation does not bode well for the future of Antony's romance with the Egyptian queen, Cleopatra.

Here, as throughout the play, Enobarbus, Antony's most loyal supporter, serves as the voice of reason; he speaks plainly, in prose rather than verse. His estrangement from Antony increases as Antony's power wanes; for the moment, however, he represents Antony's connection to the West and his political duties. Enobarbus's blunt honesty contrasts sharply with Cleopatra's theatricality.

# ACT I, SCENES IV–V; ACT II, SCENES I–II

> . . . *yet must Antony*
> *No way excuse his foils when we do bear*
> *So great weight in his lightness.*
>
> (See QUOTATIONS, p. 49)

### SUMMARY: ACT I, SCENE IV

In Rome, young Octavius Caesar complains to Lepidus, the third triumvir, that Antony has abandoned his responsibilities as a statesman and, in doing so, has also abandoned the better part of his manhood. Lepidus attempts to defend Antony, suggesting that Antony's weaknesses for fishing, drinking, and reveling are traits he inherited rather than ones he has chosen. Caesar remains unconvinced, declaring that Antony has no business enjoying himself in Egypt during a time of crisis. A messenger arrives with news that Pompey's forces are both gathering strength and finding support among those whose prior allegiance to Caesar arose from fear, not duty. Remembering Antony's valiant and unparalleled performance as a soldier, Caesar laments that Antony is not with them. He and Lepidus agree to raise an army against Pompey.

### SUMMARY: ACT I, SCENE V

Cleopatra complains to Charmian that she misses Antony. She wonders what he is doing and whether he, in turn, is thinking of her. Alexas enters and presents her with a gift from Antony: a pearl. He tells the queen that Antony kissed the gemstone upon leaving Egypt and ordered it be delivered to Cleopatra as a token of his love. Cleopatra asks if he appeared sad or happy, and she rejoices when Alexas responds that Antony seemed neither: to appear sad, Cleopatra says, might have contaminated the moods of his followers, while a happy countenance could have jeopardized his followers'

SUMMARY & ANALYSIS

belief in his resolve. Cleopatra orders Alexas to prepare twenty messengers, so that she can write to Antony on each day of his absence. She promises, if need be, to "unpeople Egypt" by turning all of its citizens into messengers (I.v.77).

## SUMMARY: ACT II, SCENE I
Pompey discusses the military situation with his lieutenants, Menecrates and Menas. He feels confident of victory against the triumvirs not only because he controls the sea and is popular with the Roman people, but also because he believes that Antony, the greatest threat to his power, is still in Egypt. Menas reports that Caesar and Lepidus have raised an army, and another soldier, Varrius, arrives to tell them that Antony has come to Rome. Menas expresses his hope that Caesar and Antony's mutual enmity will give rise to a battle between the two triumvirs, but Pompey predicts that the two will come together in order to fend off a common enemy.

## SUMMARY: ACT II, SCENE II
Lepidus tells Enobarbus that Antony should use "soft and gentle speech" when speaking to Caesar (II.ii.3). Enobarbus answers that Antony will speak as plainly and honestly as any great man should. Antony and Caesar enter with their attendants and sit down to talk. Caesar complains of the rebellion that Fulvia and Antony's brother raised against him. He asks why Antony dismissed his messengers in Alexandria and accuses Antony of failing in his obligation to provide military aid to the other triumvirs. Antony defends himself, and Maecenas, one of Caesar's companions, suggests that they put aside their bickering in order to face Pompey. Agrippa, another of Caesar's men, suggests that Antony marry Caesar's sister, Octavia. This bond, he claims, would cement the men's affection for and alliance with one another. Antony consents. Caesar and Antony shake hands, promising brotherly love, and they agree to march together toward Pompey's stronghold on Mount Misenum.

When the triumvirs disperse, Enobarbus tells Agrippa of the good life they lived in Egypt. He describes how Cleopatra first came to meet Antony, comparing the queen to Venus, the goddess of love. Antony, he maintains, will never be able to leave her, despite his marriage to Octavia.

*Age cannot wither her, nor custom stale*
*Her infinite variety. Other women cloy*
*The appetites they feed, but she makes hungry*
*Where most she satisfies.*

(See QUOTATIONS, p. 51)

---

### ANALYSIS: ACT I, SCENES IV–V; ACT II, SCENES I–II

Unlike Shakespeare's other great tragedies, *Antony and Cleopatra* is not confined to a single geographical location. Whereas *Macbeth* unfolds in Scotland and *Hamlet* in Denmark's Elsinore castle, *Antony and Cleopatra* takes the audience from one end of the Mediterranean Sea to the other in the course of a scene change. This technique is noteworthy for several reasons. First, it shows the global concerns of the play: traveling from Alexandria to Athens to Rome to Syria demonstrates the scope of the empire for which Antony, Cleopatra, and Caesar struggle. Second, the use of rapidly shifting locales shows that Shakespeare has become less interested in the deep psychological recesses that he examines in his greatest tragedies and is now addressing more public concerns. A stylistic result of Shakespeare's interest in the broader world is that *Antony and Cleopatra* lacks soliloquies, a device that Shakespeare elsewhere uses to reveal his characters' hidden thoughts to the audience.

As he shuttles the audience from Egypt to Rome, Shakespeare introduces the other members of the triumvirate who, with Antony, have ruled the Roman Empire since Julius Caesar's death. Octavius Caesar, Julius's nephew, stands in stark contrast to Antony. His first lines establish him as a man ruled by reason rather than passion, duty rather than desire. He complains that Antony neglects affairs of state in order to fish, drink, and waste the night away in revelry. Even though he lacks the military prowess that he praises in Antony, Caesar is, politically speaking, ever practical and efficient. That he disapproves so strongly of Antony's relationship with Cleopatra foreshadows the collapse of the triumvirate and forecasts Caesar's role as a worthy adversary.

Although he speaks little in Act I, scene iv, Lepidus emerges as the weakest of the three Roman leaders. Neither heroic like Antony nor politically astute like Caesar, Lepidus lacks the power and command of his fellow triumvirs. Ledipus works desperately to maintain a balance of power by keeping Caesar and Antony on amiable terms. When Caesar criticizes Antony, Lepidus urges him not to condemn their fellow triumvir so harshly, and later entreats Antony to speak gently when speaking to Caesar. The triumvirate is a triangular form of government, and it is little wonder, given the extreme weakness of one of its sides, that it soon collapses.

The focus on Roman politics and the rising threat of war in Act I, scene iv and Act II, scene i threatens to overshadow the romantic interests of the title characters. To prevent this eclipse, Shakespeare returns the audience to Egypt, in the brief interlude of Act I, scene v. This interlude reminds the audience of Cleopatra's passion and the threat it poses to the stability of the empire.

Enobarbus's lengthy description of Cleopatra in Act II, scene ii testifies to Cleopatra's power. Her beauty is so incomparable, her charms so strong that the "vilest things / Become themselves in her, that the holy priests / Bless her when she is riggish [sluttish]" (II.ii.243–245). Her talent for transforming the "vilest things" into things of beauty, and for overturning entire systems of morality so that priests alter their understanding of what is holy and what is sinful, is Cleopatra's greatest strength.

## ACT II, SCENES III–VI

### SUMMARY: ACT II, SCENE III
Antony promises Octavia that although his duties will often force him to be away from her, he will avoid the sexual indiscretions of his past. Octavia and Caesar depart, and Antony is joined by the Egyptian soothsayer, who predicts Antony's return to Egypt. Antony asks whether he or Caesar has the brighter future, and the Soothsayer answers that Caesar's fortune will rise higher. As long as Antony remains in Rome, the Soothsayer predicts, he will be overshadowed by Caesar. He advises Antony to leave plenty of space between himself and Caesar. Antony dismisses the fortune-teller but agrees with his assessment, and he resigns himself to returning to the East, where his "pleasure lies" (II.iii.38). Antony summons Ventidius, a soldier and friend, and commissions him to go east to make war against the kingdom of Parthia.

### SUMMARY: ACT II, SCENE IV
Meanwhile, Lepidus orders Maecenas and Agrippa to gather their soldiers and meet at Mount Misenum, where they shall confront Pompey's army.

## SUMMARY: ACT II, SCENE V

In Egypt, Cleopatra amuses herself with her servants Charmian and Mardian, a eunuch. As she reminisces about Antony, likening him to a fish that she has caught, a messenger arrives from Italy. Noting his unhappy expression, Cleopatra fears that Antony is dead and threatens the messenger should he deliver such unwelcome news. The messenger assures the queen that her lover is alive and well, but admits that Antony has married Octavia. Cleopatra strikes the messenger furiously, but he insists that he must tell her the truth. Cleopatra admits that it is beneath her station to treat a menial servant so viciously, but she cannot help upbraiding the man as she forces him to repeat that Antony belongs to another. She finally dismisses the messenger, then sends him orders to go and see Octavia so that he may report her features—how old she is, how she acts, even the color of her hair.

## SUMMARY: ACT II, SCENE VI

Before waging a war, Pompey and the triumvirs hold a meeting. Pompey tells Caesar, Lepidus, and Antony that he is fighting to avenge his father, whose defeat by Julius Caesar led him into Egypt, where he was killed. Antony informs Pompey that despite the latter's strength at sea, the triumvirs' army will prevail. The three offer Pompey rule over Sicily and Sardinia should he agree to rid the sea of pirates and to send payments of wheat to Rome as a tax. Pompey admits that he was ready to accept this offer until Antony offended him by refusing to acknowledge the hospitality he showed Antony's mother on her recent visit to Sicily. Antony assures Pompey that he intended to offer a gracious thanks, at which the men shake hands and make peace.

Pompey invites the Romans aboard his ship for dinner, and the triumvirs join him. Enobarbus and Menas stay behind discussing their military careers, the current political situation, and Antony's marriage to Octavia. Enobarbus repeats that he is sure Antony will inevitably return to Egypt. After the talk, the two go to dinner.

---

## ANALYSIS: ACT II, SCENES III–VI

Although the contradictory impressions we are given of the major characters may be confusing, they allow us to gain a more complex understanding of each character by seeing him or her from a variety of viewpoints. For example, in the opening scenes of the play, Demetrius and Philo complain that their general has sacrificed his better self for the sake of a gypsy's lust. Three scenes later, Caesar describes Antony's incomparable prowess in battle, confirming the audience's impression of the general's military might. When Antony appears in Act II, scene iii, however, he seems less interested in maintaining this heroic reputation than in pursuing his own pleasure. We may find it difficult to decide whether the Antony we see is the celebrated war hero or a man corrupted by his desires for fame and romance. The play does not offer simple answers to such questions, because it declines to privilege one point of view over another. Throughout, we must balance Caesar's impressions with Enobarbus's in order to reconcile Cleopatra's understanding of Antony with Antony's understanding of himself. Antony, like each character in the play, is the product of three distinct elements: what other characters think of him, what he thinks of himself, and what he does.

Although in other plays Shakespeare often limits the number of lenses through which the audience views his characters, he refrains from doing so in *Antony and Cleopatra*. Antony is not simply a hero, nor is he simply a fool who has thrown away reason and duty for love. An accurate picture of his character must incorporate both of these traits. Similarly, Cleopatra is both the regal, incomparably beautiful seductress of Enobarbus's speech and the spoiled, petty tyrant who beats her servant for delivering unwelcome news. More than any other character in the play—and perhaps in all of Shakespeare—Cleopatra assumes each of these contradictory roles with unmatched passion and flair. She is, above all else, a consummate actress, a woman whose grief over Antony's marriage to Octavia can be soothed only by the theatrics of drawing a knife on her innocent messenger. Cleopatra's over-the-top behavior may cause us to doubt the authenticity of her emotions and question whether her grief is more performance than actual feeling. But to entertain such doubts about her may be to look at the play too much from the Roman point of view. We should remember that Cleopatra is more than the harlot the Romans see when they look at her. As Enobarbus says in Act II, scene ii, Cleopatra is a woman of "infinite variety": there is room in her for both theatrical emotions and genuine love, for both stately grandeur and for girlish insecurity (II.ii.241).

The Roman characters repeatedly remark that Cleopatra's beauty is sufficient to undo otherwise indestructible men. In general, *Antony and Cleopatra* exhibits a great deal of anxiety about the power of women over men. The Romans constantly chastise Cleopatra for her ability to topple Antony's sense of reason and duty, while they expect Octavia to quell the animosity between Antony and Caesar by serving to "knit [their] hearts / With an unslipping knot" (II.ii.132–133). Notably, both the blame for men's downfalls and the hope for their recovery are burdens placed on women.

## ACT II, SCENE VII; ACT III, SCENES I–III

> Most noble Antony,
> Let not the piece of virtue which is set
> Betwixt us as the cement of our love
> To keep it builded, be the ram to batter
> The fortress of it. . . .
>
> (See QUOTATIONS, p. 52)

SUMMARY & ANALYSIS

SUMMARY: ACT II, SCENE VII

A group of servants discusses Pompey's dinner party, commenting on Lepidus's drunkenness in particular. Pompey enters with his guests as Antony discusses the Nile River. Lepidus babbles on about crocodiles, which, according to popular belief, formed spontaneously out of the river mud. Lepidus asks Antony to describe the crocodile, and Antony responds with a humorously circular and meaningless definition: "It is shaped, sir, like itself, and is as broad as it hath breadth" (II.vii.39–40). Menas pulls Pompey aside to suggest that they set sail and kill the three triumvirs while they are still drunk and onboard the boat, thus delivering control of the Western world into Pompey's hands. Pompey rails against Menas for sharing this plan with him. Were the deed done without his knowledge, Pompey says, he would have praised it, but now that he knows, it would violate his honor. In an angry aside, Menas expresses his disappointment with Pompey and swears that he will leave his master's service. Meanwhile, the triumvirs and their host continue their drunken revelry, eventually joining hands, dancing, and singing before they leave the ship and stumble off to bed.

SUMMARY: ACT III, SCENE I

Ventidius, fighting for Antony, defeats the Parthians, killing their king's son. One of Ventidius's soldiers urges him to push on into Parthia and win more glory, but Ventidius says he should not. If he were too successful in war, he explains, he would fall out of Antony's favor and not be able to advance as a member of Antony's forces. Instead, Ventidius halts his army and writes to Antony, informing him of his victory.

## SUMMARY: ACT III, SCENE II
Agrippa and Enobarbus discuss the current state of affairs: Pompey has gone, Octavia and Caesar are saddened by their nearing separation, and Lepidus is still sick from his night of heavy drinking. Agrippa and Enobarbus mock Lepidus, the weakest of the three triumvirs, who trips over himself in order to stay on good terms with both Antony and Caesar. A trumpet blares, and Lepidus, Antony, and Caesar enter. Caesar bids farewell to Antony and his sister, urging his new brother-in-law never to mistreat Octavia and thereby drive a wedge between himself and Antony. Antony implores Caesar not to offend him, making assurances that he will not justify Caesar's fears. Antony and Octavia depart, leaving Lepidus and Caesar in Rome.

## SUMMARY: ACT III, SCENE III
Cleopatra's messenger returns to report on Antony's bride. He tells Cleopatra that Octavia is shorter than she and that Octavia has a low voice and is rather lifeless. This news pleases Cleopatra, who delights in thinking that Antony's bride is stupid and short. She decides that, given Octavia's lack of positive attributes, Antony cannot possibly enjoy being with her for long. She promises to reward the messenger for his good service, showers him with gold, and asks him not to think of her too harshly for her past treatment of him. She then tells Charmian that Antony will almost certainly return to her.

## ANALYSIS: ACT II, SCENE VII; ACT III, SCENES I–III
Both Ventidius's speech after the victory over Parthia and the events of the party challenge and complicate our understanding of honor. Ventidius's contemplation of his performance in battle in Act II, scene i offers a definition of honor based on prowess in battle. Ventidius explains that it would not be honorable to conquer too extensively, since eclipsing his captain's fame would reflect poorly on himself. Whereas Pompey's definition of honor has to do with appearance, Ventidius's has to do with ambition. Ultimately, it is clear that Ventidius contemplates his honorable leading of the army as a way of achieving greater status; he ends his speech describing the perils of overachievement with the words, "I could do more to

do Antonius good, / But 'twould offend him, and in his offence / Should my performance perish" (III.i.25–27). Ventidius seems to care at least as much about Antony's opinion of his performance in war as about his sense of honor.

Pompey's sense of honor, however, is based on surface appearances. His desire that the triumvirate be deposed might easily be seen as dishonorable, since he appears to be making peace with them. However, he believes that he retains his honor by not acting on his dishonorable feelings. When Menas suggests that he be allowed to assassinate the triumvirs in order to deliver world power into Pompey's hands, Pompey's reasoning for condemning Menas's plan shows that it is not the act itself that would challenge Pompey's public honor, but rather its appearance:

> Ah, this thou shouldst have done
> And not have spoke on't. In me 'tis villainy,
> In thee 't had been good service. Thou must know
> 'Tis not my profit that does lead mine honour;
> Mine honour it. Repent that e'er thy tongue
> Hath so betrayed thine act. Being done unknown,
> I should have found it afterwards well done,
> But must condemn it now.
>
> (II.vii.70–77)

Pompey does not condemn the assassination of his unsuspecting— indeed, helplessly drunken—guests as treacherous or morally irresponsible. Instead, he complains that Menas shared the plan with him, a divulgence that, if discovered, would affect the way that the world sees him. Pompey would no longer be looked upon as an honorable man if he murdered his guests. In a play that invests so much in surface, even qualities such as honor and nobility have more to do with spectacle than with deeper human emotions.

Lepidus's drunkenness symbolizes his physical and political weakness: indeed, he makes only one more appearance before being eliminated by Caesar, fulfilling the servants' prophesy that even world leaders can be easily overthrown. That Caesar proves the wind that blows Lepidus (and eventually Antony) down should not come as any surprise, given his behavior aboard Pompey's ship. Caesar alone manages to elevate duty above pleasure; he alone interrupts the night's carousing to remind Antony that their more serious business conflicts with the extended revelry. Perhaps the most telling phrase Antony utters in this scene comes as he tries to persuade Caesar to forget duty for the night. While urging his men to drink until "the conquering wine hath steeped our sense / In soft and delicate Lethe," he bids Caesar to "[b]e a child o'th' time"—to live, in other words, strictly for the moment, for the pleasure of the present (II.vii.94–103). Antony's propensity to live according to the moment, with little regard for the future or the consequences of his actions, is one of the greatest factors in his demise.

## ACT III, SCENES IV–VII

### SUMMARY: ACT III, SCENE IV
Antony complains to Octavia that since departing Rome, Caesar has not only waged war against Pompey but has also belittled Antony in public. Octavia urges Antony not to believe everything he hears, and she pleads with him to keep the peace with her brother. Were Antony and Caesar to fight, Octavia laments, she would not know whether to support her brother or her husband. Antony tells her that he must do what needs to be done to preserve his honor, without which he would be nothing. Nevertheless, he sends her to Rome to make peace again between Caesar and himself. Meanwhile, he prepares for war against Pompey.

### SUMMARY: ACT III, SCENE V
Enobarbus converses with Eros, another friend of Antony. The two discuss Caesar's defeat of Pompey's army and the murder of Pompey. Eros reports that Caesar made use of Lepidus's forces, but then, after their victory, denied Lepidus his share of the spoils. In fact, Caesar has accused the triumvir of plotting against him and has thrown him into prison. Enobarbus reports that Antony's navy is ready to sail for Italy and Caesar.

### SUMMARY: ACT III, SCENE VI
Back in Rome, Caesar rails against Antony. He tells Agrippa and Maecenas that Antony has gone to Egypt to sit alongside Cleopatra as her king. He has given her rule over much of the Middle East, making her absolute queen of lower Syria, Cyprus, and Lydia. Caesar reports that Antony is displeased that he has not yet been allotted a fair portion of the lands that Caesar wrested from Pompey and Lepidus. He will divide his lot, he says, if Antony responds in kind

and grants him part of Armenia and other kingdoms that Antony conquered. No sooner does Maecenas predict that Antony will never concede to those terms than Octavia enters. Caesar laments that the woman travels so plainly, without the fanfare that should attend the wife of Antony. Caesar reveals to her that Antony has joined Cleopatra in Egypt, where he has assembled a large alliance to fight Rome. Octavia is heartbroken, and Maecenas assures her that she has the sympathy of every Roman citizen.

## SUMMARY: ACT III, SCENE VII

Cleopatra plans to go into battle alongside Antony and responds angrily to Enobarbus's suggestion that her presence will be a distraction. Enobarbus tries to dissuade her, but she dismisses his objections. Antony tells his general, Camidius, that he will meet Caesar at sea. Camidius and Enobarbus object, pointing out that while they have superiority on land, Caesar's naval fleet is much stronger. Antony, however, refuses to listen. Cleopatra maintains that her fleet of sixty ships will win the battle. Antony leaves to prepare the navy, despite the protests of a soldier who begs him to forgo a doomed sea battle and advocates fighting on foot. After the general and the queen exit, Camidius complains that they are all "women's men," ruled by Cleopatra (III.vii.70). He comments on the speed of Caesar's approach, then goes to prepare the land defenses.

---

## ANALYSIS: ACT III, SCENES IV–VII

Caesar's description of Antony and Cleopatra in Act III, scene vi shows the play's preoccupation with the sexualized East. The scene recalls an earlier speech by Enobarbus in which he states that the Egyptian queen floats down the Nile on a glittering throne. Just as Cleopatra and her barge are a vision of decadent beauty in the earlier speech, so is the image of the queen and her lover in the marketplace of Alexandria. Caesar's exchange with Maecenas underscores the spectacular nature of Antony and Cleopatra's appearance:

> CAESAR: Contemning Rome, he has done all this and more
> In Alexandria. Here's the manner of't:
> I' th' market place on a tribunal silvered,
> Cleopatra and himself in chairs of gold
> Were publicly enthroned. . . .

SUMMARY & ANALYSIS

MAECENAS: This in the public eye?

CAESAR: I' th' common showplace, where they exercise.
. . .

> She
> In th'habiliments of the goddess Isis
> That day appeared, and oft before gave audience
> (III.vi.2–19)

*Antony and Cleopatra* draws distinctions between the West and the East by illustrating the West as sober, military, and masculine, and the East as exotic, pleasure-loving, and sexual. In this scene, it is not only the public appearance of Antony with a woman not his wife that shocks Maecenas, Caesar, and Agrippa, but also the decadence with which they appear. While the military men confer in the West regarding the machinations of war, Antony's life in the East is represented as focused on sensual pleasures, both with Cleopatra and within the wealth and splendor of her kingdom.

This passage also confirms Cleopatra's theatricality and the world's preoccupation with spectacle. Spectacle is of supreme importance throughout the play, as Caesar again makes clear when he complains to Octavia about her lack of it. Bent on keeping the peace between her husband and brother, Octavia arrives in Rome without any of the fanfare or trappings that would indicate her station. Caesar insists that the

> wife of Antony
> Should have an army for an usher, and
> The neighs of horse to tell of her approach
> Long ere she did appear.
> (III.vi.43–46)

Caesar likens Octavia's appearance to that of a common maid going to market. Caesar links spectacle with power: the greater the display, the more substantial and genuine the power behind it. Caesar returns to this line of thinking at the play's end when he plans to display Cleopatra on the streets of Rome as a testament to the indomitable strength of his empire. Here we see the equation between spectacle and power in reverse: Octavia's unheralded arrival in Rome betrays what Caesar knows too well—his sister has little, if any, power over a husband whose heart visibly belongs to Egypt.

SUMMARY & ANALYSIS

The romance between Antony and Cleopatra is different from the romance between some of Shakespeare's other major characters because it focuses on how the two mesh with larger historical and social dramas. Whereas *Romeo and Juliet,* for instance, largely chronicles the private moments of its teenaged protagonists, following the couple as they steal moments together at a crowded party or on a moonlit balcony, *Antony and Cleopatra*'s concerns are public rather than private. Antony's return to and reconciliation with Cleopatra take place offstage, as do all of the more private moments of their relationship. What earns stage time in this play are not the muted whispers of discreet lovers but the grand performances of lovers who live in, and play for, the public eye. Love, in *Antony and Cleopatra,* seems less a product of the bedroom than of political alliance, for we are always aware of the public consequences of the couple's affair. When Caesar laments that Antony has given up his empire for a whore, we understand the enormous impact—both civic and geographic—that the lovers' affair will have on the world. Kingdoms stand to be built on the foundation of Antony and Cleopatra's love or crumble under its weight.

## ACT III, SCENES VIII–XIII

### SUMMARY: ACT III, SCENE VIII
Caesar orders his army to hold off its attack until the sea battle ends.

### SUMMARY: ACT III, SCENE IX
Antony instructs Enobarbus to set their squadrons on a hillside, which will allow them to view the battle at sea.

### SUMMARY: ACT III, SCENE X
Enobarbus describes the sea fight he has just witnessed: Antony's forces were winning the battle until Cleopatra's ship fled without warning and Antony followed her. The fleet was thrown into confusion, and the victory went to Caesar. Antony's soldiers are sickened by the sight, one of them declaring that he has never seen anything so shameful. Camidius defects to Caesar's side, bringing his army and following the lead of six of Antony's royal allies, but Enobarbus, against his better judgment, remains loyal to his general.

### SUMMARY: ACT III, SCENE XI

Deeply ashamed of his performance in battle, Antony berates himself, ordering his servants to leave the service of such an unworthy master. He urges them to abandon Antony as Antony has abandoned his nobler self. When Cleopatra enters, she finds her lover distraught and alone. She tries to comfort him, but Antony can remind her only of his valiant past: it was he who won fierce battles, who dealt with the treacheries of Cassius and Brutus. But now, he determines, such events do not matter. He asks Cleopatra why she has led him into infamy, and she begs his forgiveness, saying that she never dreamed that he would follow her retreat. He asks her how she could doubt that he would follow her, when his heart was tied to her rudder. Antony complains that he must now seek young Caesar's pardon, but unable to bear the sight of the queen's sorrow, he forgives her. As Antony kisses Cleopatra, he remarks that even her mere kiss repays him for his shame.

### SUMMARY: ACT III, SCENE XII

Caesar is with Dolabella and Thidias, two of his supporters, when Antony's ambassador arrives with his master's request: Antony asks to be allowed to live in Egypt or, barring that, to "breathe between the heavens and earth, / A private man in Athens" (III.xii.14–15). The ambassador further delivers Cleopatra's request that Egypt be passed on to her heirs. Caesar dismisses Antony's requests but declares that Cleopatra will have a fair hearing so long as she expels Antony from Egypt or executes him. He sends Thidias to lure Cleopatra to accept these terms, hoping that she will betray her lover.

### SUMMARY: ACT III, SCENE XIII

Enobarbus tells Cleopatra that the defeat was not her fault since Antony could have chosen to follow reason rather than lust. The ambassador returns with Caesar's message: Antony declares that he will challenge his rival to one-on-one combat. Enobarbus meditates on such a course of action, but decides that if he remains loyal to Antony he might be able to attack Caesar, if Caesar kills Antony. Meanwhile, Thidias arrives to tell Cleopatra that Caesar will show her mercy if she will relinquish Antony. The queen concedes that she embraced Antony more out of fear than love and declares Caesar a god to whom she will bow down. Just then, Antony enters in a fury and demands that Thidias be whipped. He then turns to Cleopatra and rails at her for betraying him. The queen protests that she would

SUMMARY & ANALYSIS

never betray him, which satisfies Antony. Antony's fleet has reassembled, and much of his land forces remain intact, ready to attack Caesar again. Enobarbus, who has observed this scene, decides that he has been faithful to Antony long enough. He feels that Antony's mind is slipping and that he must abandon his master.

---

### ANALYSIS: ACT III, SCENES VIII–XIII

Act III, scenes viii–x show that narrative time and chronological time occur at much different paces in *Antony and Cleopatra*. In the space of three scenes, we witness the full battle of Actium. We see Caesar, then Antony, prepare for battle and know the outcome of their meeting within the first four lines of Act III, scene x. In other sections of the play, the same number of scenes conveys less information and covers much less time. The rapid progression of these scenes attests to the ease with which time can be compressed onstage: in a matter of minutes, an entire naval battle is waged and won.

What Enobarbus witnesses certainly complicates our perception of Antony, demonstrating that his failures take place not just in his private affiliations but in his public life as well. Although by Caesar's and even by his own account he has neglected his duties to Rome, Antony has remained a fierce and respected soldier: his quietly threatening presence, as much as any offer of Sicily and Sardinia, persuades young Pompey to accept the triumvir's offer of peace. Indeed, until this point, the blemishes on Antony's character have been of a more personal nature: although he is twice an adulterer, although he has risked the security of the empire in order to partake in the pleasures of Egypt, his military prowess has never been in question. His retreat, however, conflicts with his values, as he is a man whose honor rests almost exclusively in his performance as a soldier.

A number of critics have attacked this moment in the play, asserting that such a retreat by an experienced general is unbelievable. To condemn or dismiss this scene for its lack of realism, however, misses the point for several reasons. First, by failing to allow Antony to be both the famed soldier and the distracted lover, to be both noble and irresponsible, one simplifies and diminishes his character. Second, the lost navy battle is more crucial on a symbolic than a literal level, for Antony's decision to flee encapsulates the climactic neglect of duty that haunts him throughout the play.

SUMMARY & ANALYSIS

The aftermath of the battle shows that Antony is struggling with divided, competing identities. His lament that he has fled from himself shows that his character has developed beyond his own understanding. The self he believes he has fled is the military hero; the self he now confronts is a man whose heart can lead him into defeat as surely as his reason has led him into victory. The play, however, refuses to side with Antony in his argument against himself. We may share in Enobarbus's disapproval of his commander's performance, but surely we still view Antony as a worthy and sympathetic character. Indeed, the fallen general's plea to Cleopatra makes it impossible to respond to him with simple contempt:

> Egypt, thou knew'st too well
> My heart was to thy rudder tied by th'strings,
> And thou shouldst tow me after. O'er my spirit
> Thy full supremacy thou knew'st, and that
> Thy beck might from the bidding of the gods
> Command me.
>
> (III.xi.56–61)

Antony's willingness to accept defeat out of his great love for Cleopatra does not make him a two-dimensional character, nor does it make him reprehensible to us. In fact, his flaws may be exactly what we respond to, since they highlight that he is human, riddled with weaknesses despite his famous strengths.

## ACT IV, SCENES I–VIII

### SUMMARY: ACT IV, SCENE I
Caesar, encamped near the Egyptian capital of Alexandria, receives Antony's challenge and laughs at it. Maecenas counsels him to take advantage of Antony's rage, for "[n]ever anger / Made good guard for itself" (IV.i.9–10). Caesar prepares his army—swelled by deserters from his enemy's troops—and plans to crush Antony for good.

### SUMMARY: ACT IV, SCENE II
Enobarbus brings word to Antony that Caesar has refused to fight him. Antony asks why, and Enobarbus suggests that Caesar is so sure of success that one-on-one combat seems unfair. Antony declares that he will fight the next day, whether it brings him victory

or death. He thanks his servants for their faithful service and warns them that this night might be his last night with them. They begin to weep, and Enobarbus, with tears in his eyes, rebukes Antony for such a morbid speech. Antony says that he did not mean to cause sorrow, and, as he leads them off toward a bountiful feast, urges them to enjoy their evening together.

### SUMMARY: ACT IV, SCENE III
That night, Antony's soldiers hear strange music resounding from somewhere underground. They whisper that it is the music of Hercules, the god after whom Antony modeled himself and who they believe now abandons him.

### SUMMARY: ACT IV, SCENE IV
The following day, Eros arms Antony for battle, and Cleopatra insists on helping. Antony feels confident about the coming fight, promising Cleopatra that anyone who attempts to undo his armor before he is ready to remove it and rest will confront his rage. An armed soldier enters and reports that a thousand others stand ready for Antony's command. Antony bids Cleopatra adieu, kisses her, and leads his men into battle.

### SUMMARY: ACT IV, SCENE V
Preparing for battle, Antony admits he wishes he had taken the earlier opportunity to oppose Caesar on land. A soldier comments that had he done so, he would still count Enobarbus as an ally. This report is the first Antony has heard of his most trusted friend's desertion, and the news shocks him. At first he does not believe it, but Eros then points to the "chests and treasure" Enobarbus left behind (IV.v.10). Antony orders soldiers to deliver Enobarbus's possessions to him, along with "gentle adieus and greetings," and laments that his "fortunes have / Corrupted honest men" (IV.v.14–17).

### SUMMARY: ACT IV, SCENE VI
Caesar, feeling certain of his victory, orders Agrippa to begin the battle. Caesar orders that the front lines be fitted with soldiers who have deserted Antony, so that Antony will feel like he that he is wasting his efforts fighting himself. Enobarbus receives the treasure and is overcome by guilt, realizing that he has become a common traitor. Deciding that he would rather die than fight against Antony, he declares himself a villain and goes to seek out a ditch in which to die.

SUMMARY & ANALYSIS

SUMMARY: ACT IV, SCENE VII
Agrippa calls for his troops to retreat, declaring that the power of Antony's forces has exceeded his expectations.

SUMMARY: ACT IV, SCENE VIII
Antony's men win the battle and retake Alexandria with a fierce display of force. Scarus receives a fantastic wound but will not relent, begging Antony for the chance to chase after the retreating army.

---

ANALYSIS: ACT IV, SCENES I–VIII
Because the play's dramatic structure suggests that the battle in Act IV will be climactic and probably result in Antony's death, Antony's victory in these scenes is surprising and makes the plot much less predictable. After Antony's flight from battle in Act III, and after Cleopatra's apparent willingness to betray her lover, all seems lost for the lovers. Indeed, the opening scenes of Act IV confirm and build upon this impression. Caesar rejects Antony's proposal for hand-to-hand combat with such assurance that we feel that there is something prophetic in the line "Know that tomorrow the last of many battles / We mean to fight" (IV.i.11–12). Antony, seemingly undone by the treachery of his own behavior, manages to burden his men with sadness rather than rouse them for battle, while several soldiers hear an otherworldly music they believe portends the destruction of the once great general and his forces.

Not only do these scenes redirect our expectations, they also suggest different interpretations of Antony's and Cleopatra's characters. Up to this point in the play, the two lovers seem to have been so absorbed in their own romance that they have allowed nations to go to war. A decidedly Roman perspective has dominated the presentation of Cleopatra as a wanton gypsy and Antony as her fool. The day of battle, however, brings victory to Antony and, at least for a moment, restores him to good fortune. Fighting a vicious and bloody fight, Antony displays the martial abilities that have forged his reputation, and he wins the battle. In these scenes both Antony and Cleopatra display depths of character that cannot be reduced to the respective fool and strumpet. The boldest, most incontrovertible display of the honor for which Antony is famed comes not in battle but in his decision to return to Enobarbus his abandoned treasures.

Enobarbus's defection to Caesar's side underscores one of the play's main concerns: the mutability of human character. Once one of Antony's most confident and self-assured comrades, Enobarbus becomes a man ruined by guilt over his disloyalty. The completeness of his change of heart is called into question, however, when he declares that he will go off to die in a ditch, because the latter part of his life has been foul. Although he has changed sides, he refuses to fight against Antony. Enobarbus lacks the distance necessary to see his life as a whole, and to understand the honorability of his past actions. He concentrates only on recent dishonorable actions, and so determines to die. But our understanding of Enobarbus must incorporate his former and present selves, the best and the foulest.

## ACT IV, SCENES IX–XV

> *Nay, weep not, gentle Eros. There is left us*
> *Ourselves to end ourselves.*
>
> (See QUOTATIONS, p. 53)

### SUMMARY: ACT IV, SCENE IX
Antony returns from war, vowing to destroy Caesar's army completely on the following day. He praises his soldiers for their valor and commands them to regale their families with tales of the day's battle. When Cleopatra enters, Antony declares his love for her. He announces that she is the only thing that can pierce his armor and reach his heart. Antony asks Cleopatra to commend Scarus, one of his bravest soldiers. The queen promises the man a suit of golden armor that once belonged to a king. Antony leads his troops and his lover in a triumphant march through the streets of Alexandria to mark the joyous occasion.

### SUMMARY: ACT IV, SCENE X
Caesar's sentries discuss the coming battle as Enobarbus berates himself nearby. Unaware that he is being watched, Enobarbus rails against his life, wishing for its end and hoping that history will mark him as a traitor and a fugitive. After he collapses, the sentries decide to rouse him but discover that he has died. Because he is an important man, they bear his body to their camp.

### SUMMARY: ACT IV, SCENE XI
Antony determines that Caesar means to attack him by sea and declares himself ready. He wishes his enemy were equipped to fight in fire or air, swearing he would meet him in those places if he could.

## Summary: Act IV, scene xii
Caesar holds his armies back, preparing to attack Antony at sea.

## Summary: Act IV, scene xiii
Anthony has gone with Scarus to watch the naval battle. Scarus, in an aside, condemns Cleopatra's fleet as weak, and laments that the soothsayers refuse to share their knowledge regarding the battle's outcome. Antony watches as the Egyptian fleet betrays him and defects to Caesar. Realizing his predicament, Antony commands Scarus to order his army to flee. Alone, the general blames Cleopatra as a deadly enchantress who has beguiled him to a state of absolute loss. When the queen enters, Antony drives her away, threatening to kill her for her betrayal.

## Summary: Act IV, scene xiv
Cleopatra returns to her maids with tales of Antony's murderous rage. Charmian suggests that her mistress lock herself in a monument and send Antony word that she has killed herself, to quell his anger. Abiding by the plan, she bids Mardian deliver the news to Antony and asks him to return with word of her lover's reaction.

## Summary: Act IV, scene xv
Antony arms himself to kill his lover, telling Eros that he no longer knows who he is now that Cleopatra's love has proven false. Mardian arrives with his false report of the queen's death, adding that her last words were "'Antony! most noble Antony!'" (IV.xv.30). Antony tells Eros to unarm. Overcome with remorse, he declares that he will join Cleopatra in death and beg her forgiveness for thinking him false. He asks Eros to kill him. Horrified, Eros refuses, but Antony reminds him of the pledge he made long ago to follow even Antony's most extreme wishes. Eros relents. He prepares to stab Antony but stabs himself instead. Antony praises his soldier's honor and says he must learn from this example. He falls on his own sword but fails to kill himself. A group of guardsmen refuses to finish the task, and Diomedes, a servant of Cleopatra, reports that the queen is alive and well. It is too late, however, to save Antony's life. Dying, Antony commands his guards to bear his body to Cleopatra.

SUMMARY & ANALYSIS

SUMMARY & ANALYSIS

ANALYSIS: ACT IV, SCENES IX–XV

In Act IV, scene xv, Antony, who has been betrayed by his lover and has lost the war to Caesar, offers one of the play's most profound reflections on the connection between character and circumstance: "Here I am Antony, / Yet cannot hold this visible shape, my knave" (IV.xv.13–14). As his fortune changes from good to bad, so, he believes, his character slips from honorable to dishonorable. He likens himself to a cloud that shifts from one shape into another. Given the play's investment in spectacle—neither love nor war truly matters unless one has something to *show* for them—Antony's disturbance at being unable to hold a "visible shape" is particularly interesting. His honor, it seems, is primarily a function of whether the world sees him as honorable. When it fails to do so, Antony no longer fits into it. His rigid definition of himself as a victorious general and as Cleopatra's lover betrays his Roman sensibilities, which cannot and will not allow him to assume the contradictory roles of the conqueror and the conquered. He will, he decides, either be the hero or cease to exist at all by killing himself. His statement "Here I am Antony" reflects his search for a glimpse of his former, simpler self: the indomitable hero who will put an end to his life. Thus, he thankfully notes to Eros, all that remains to him is suicide.

Once the second sea battle is lost, the play belongs to Antony until his death—Cleopatra recedes, as does Caesar. In the scenes leading up to his death, Antony's feelings of betrayal, regret, and, ultimately, love give way to some of the finest language in the play.

> Oh, sun, thy uprise shall I see no more:
> Fortune and Antony part here; even here
> Do we shake hands. All come to this? The hearts
> That spanieled me at heels, to whom I gave
> Their wishes, do discandy, melt their sweets
> On blossoming Caesar, and this pine is barked
> That over topped them all.
>
> (IV.xiii.18–24)

Here, as Antony bids goodbye to "Fortune," he comes to an important realization from which he cannot recover. Comparing himself to a tree that once towered above all others, he now feels that Cleopatra's inconstant love, which once "spanieled" at his heels, has stripped him of his bark. This metaphor expresses that he feels raw, unprotected, and doomed to die. Cleopatra enters soon after Antony delivers these lines, and he scares her away with vicious threats. More than anger, however, Antony feels a keen sense of loss. He laments, "I made these wars for . . . the Queen— / Whose heart I thought I had, for she had mine, / Which . . . had annexed unto't / A million more, now lost" (IV.xv.15–18). This utterance of regret confirms Antony's lost sense of self: he no longer possesses either of the identities—military giant or lover of Cleopatra—that have defined him so well.

The news of Cleopatra's suicide suffices to cool Antony's temper and returns him to thoughts of reconciliation. By killing himself, Antony envisions joining his love in the afterlife: "I come, my queen . . . / Where souls do couch on flowers we'll hand in hand, / And with our sprightly port make the ghosts gaze" (IV.xv.50–52). This consummation in death of their love moves the couple toward its ultimate victory over Caesar and the Roman Empire.

## ACT IV, SCENE XVI–ACT V, SCENE I

### SUMMARY: ACT IV, SCENE XVI

From atop the monument with her maids, Charmian and Iras, Cleopatra declares that she will never leave her hiding place. Diomedes appears below and calls up to her that Antony's guard has brought the wounded Antony. The lovers call to one another. Antony says that he is dying and wishes to embrace her one last time. She replies that she dares not come down from her monument, lest she be captured by Caesar and paraded through the streets as a prisoner of war. Instead, Cleopatra asks the soldiers to heave Antony up to her. As they do so, Cleopatra notes that the strength of Antony's body has turned to heaviness. She pulls him to her and kisses him, the onlookers declaring this intimacy "a heavy sight" (IV.xvi.42). Antony advises the queen to cast herself upon Caesar's mercy, trusting in the honesty of Caesar's friend Proculeius. He then recalls his own greatness and says that he will die gloriously, "a Roman by a Roman / Valiantly vanquished" (IV.xvi.59–60). He dies, and Cleopatra curses the world as a suddenly very dull place. Without Antony, she feels that neither life nor she herself is the least bit remarkable: she might as well be a "maid that milks / And does the meanest chores" (IV.xvi.76–77). After her maids revive her from a fainting spell, Cleopatra decides that they must bury Antony in Roman fashion and then help her seek her own death.

## Summary: Act V, scene i

Caesar orders Dolabella to deliver to Antony a command for his surrender. After Dolabella leaves, Decretas, one of Antony's men, enters carrying Antony's sword. When Caesar asks why the man would dare appear before him in such a way, Decretas explains that he was a loyal follower of Antony's and now wishes to serve Caesar as faithfully. Caesar questions the meaning of this reversal, and Decretas explains that his master is dead, taken from this world by the same noble hands that committed the brave deeds for which Antony is so renowned. Caesar remarks that the passing of such a great man ought to be marked by great tumult and mourning—after all, the death of Antony, as one of the two triumvirs, "is not a single doom" but the end of one-half of the world (V.i.18). Agrippa notes the irony of their mourning Antony's death after having fought him so fiercely. Caesar and his men agree that Antony was a great man, and Caesar declares it proper to mourn him.

A messenger arrives from Cleopatra to ask what Caesar intends for the queen. Caesar promises to be honorable and kind to her, and dispatches Cleopatra's messenger with assurances, bidding her to be of good heart. Although Caesar tells Cleopatra that he intends to cause her no shame, he plans to force her to live in Rome, where she will be his eternal triumph. Toward this end, he orders some of his men, led by Proculeius, to prevent Cleopatra from committing suicide and thus robbing him of renown.

---

## Analysis: Act IV, scene xvi–Act V, scene i

Antony's understanding of himself cannot incorporate military defeat or romantic betrayal: he would rather die thinking of himself as a hero and conqueror than live a life of shifting (and potentially ignoble) identities. Thus, Antony's suicide is his last—and most lasting—triumph. In dying, Antony not only understands himself as a victor but also convinces the world of his honor and might. Cleopatra agrees with her lover that no one but he is worthy to conquer Antony, and even Caesar musters awe for his vanquished foe, remarking that Antony's death represents a calamity for half the world. Whether we share Caesar's awe, we cannot help but feel sympathy for the dying Antony. His love for Cleopatra has led him to destroy himself, but his love does not wane. Antony's steadfastness contributes to the depth of his tragedy. He spends his dying breath advising Cleopatra to trust in Caesar's mercy and Proculeius's care.

SUMMARY & ANALYSIS

Antony is a Roman nobly vanquished by a Roman, but he is still a misguided politician and lover (IV.xvi.59–60). The sword on which he falls does not excise the blemish of his soldier's opening remark: he remains both a fool *and* a hero. Just as any complete understanding of the play must take into account the competing forces of East and West, reason and passion, discussion of Antony's character must account for both his glory and his baseness.

Even in the face of her lover's death, Cleopatra is unable to stop performing. For Cleopatra, the public display of emotions corresponds directly to their genuineness; preparing to meet Antony's death, the queen resolves that "[o]ur size of sorrow, / Proportioned to our cause, must be as great / As that which makes it" (IV.xvi.4–6). These words echo her opening lines, in which she begs Antony to outdo himself and all others with professions of love. The importance of performance becomes clear as Antony begins to speak his dying words:

ANTONY: I am dying, Egypt, dying.
            Give me some wine, and let me speak a little.
CLEOPATRA: No, let me speak, and let me rail so high
            That the false hussy Fortune break her wheel,
            Provoked by my offence.

                                (IV.xvi.43–47)

Here, Cleopatra's self-awareness in her role as grief-stricken lover rises to a near comedic level when she interrupts Antony as he tries to deliver his last words.

## ACT V, SCENE II

> *Antony*
> *Shall be brought drunken forth, and I shall see*
> *Some squeaking Cleopatra boy my greatness*
> *I' th' posture of a whore.*
>
> (See QUOTATIONS, p. 54)

### SUMMARY

Proculeius arrives at the queen's monument and asks Cleopatra's terms for giving herself up to Caesar. Cleopatra remembers that Antony told her to trust Proculeius and tells the Roman she hopes the emperor will allow her son to rule Egypt. Proculeius assures her that

Caesar will be generous and says that Caesar will soon repay her supplication with kindness. Meanwhile, his soldiers, having slipped into the monument, move to seize Cleopatra. The queen draws a dagger, hoping to kill herself before being taken captive, but Proculeius disarms her. He orders the soldiers to guard the queen until Caesar arrives, and Cleopatra cries that she will never allow herself to be carried through Rome as a trophy of the empire's triumph.

Dolabella arrives and takes over for Proculeius. The queen converses with him, discussing her dreams (in which she sees a heroic vision of Antony), and then persuades Dolabella to admit that Caesar plans to display her as a prisoner of war. Caesar arrives and promises to spare Cleopatra's children and treat her well if she does not kill herself. She gives him a scroll that hands over all her treasure to him—or so she says. When Cleopatra asks her treasurer, Seleucus, to confirm that she has given Caesar everything, Seleucus contradicts her. Cleopatra rails against the treachery of her servant, but Caesar comforts her. He assures her that he does not desire her wealth, since he is far greater than a mere merchant. When Caesar leaves, Cleopatra admits to her maids that she doubts his intentions, remarking to her companions that he is charming her with words, and Iras and Charmian encourage her to follow her plan toward death. Confirming Cleopatra's doubts, Dolabella admits that Caesar means to convey the queen to Rome and encourages the queen to respond to this news as she sees fit.

Rather than succumb to the infamy of being a spectacle for the entertainment of filthy Roman crowds, Cleopatra resolves to kill herself. She would rather die than see herself imitated by a boy actor, who would portray her as a common whore. She orders Charmian and Iras to dress her in her most queenly robes. When they have done so, she admits into her presence a clown, who brings her a basket of figs that contains asps—poisonous snakes.

Dressed in her finest royal garments, Cleopatra kisses her maids goodbye. Iras falls dead, and Cleopatra takes a snake from the basket and presses it to her breast. She applies another asp to her arm, and dies. As the guards rush in to discover the dead queen, Charmian presses the snake to herself and joins her mistress in death. Dolabella enters, followed by Caesar. They realize the manner of the suicide, and Caesar orders Cleopatra to be buried next to Antony in a public funeral.

## ANALYSIS

If the Roman Empire represents reason and order, then it is possible to view Antony's suicide as a result of his Western sensibilities, which prevent him from understanding himself as anything other than a typical Roman hero. Cleopatra's death follows her lover's, and though her suicide might, as she hopes, bring about her reunion with Antony, her reasons for killing herself are decidedly non-Western. In the play's simplified, romanticized conception of East and West, Cleopatra's application of the deadly snakes is a product of her Eastern sensibilities. Whereas Antony's Roman mind cannot conceive of Antony as a vanquished general or jilted lover, Cleopatra will not allow her multifaceted identity to be stripped to one of its simplest, basest components. Throughout the course of the play, her character has been as shifting as the clouds that Antony describes in Act IV, scene xv. Her love and her grief are, at turns, convincing and suspiciously theatrical. She gives her heart to Antony and then, with no warning, her political allegiance to his enemy. She treats her servants with surpassing kindness and then, moments later, beats them ruthlessly. Cleopatra is decidedly inconstant; yet, she is never anything less than herself: passionate, grand, and over the top. Thus, she refuses to allow the Romans to reduce her to their understanding of her, to parade her through their filthy streets as some prepubescent boy mimics her greatness: "I' th' posture of a whore" (V.ii.217). By killing herself, Cleopatra remains Cleopatra.

Of the many performances Cleopatra stages throughout the play, her triumph over the Romans in Act V, scene ii is, without doubt, her greatest. Here, her complex character seems to have secret longings and undisclosed motivations. For instance, she seems resigned to joining Antony in death at the end of Act IV, scene xvi, concurring with him that suicide and resolve are their only friends. We may wonder, then, why Cleopatra bothers convincing Dolabella to reveal Caesar's desire to turn her into the empire's trophy. Caesar's intentions wouldn't matter to someone as committed to dying as Cleopatra says she is. Similarly, her motivations for trying to preserve her possessions from Caesar are unclear. Perhaps she entertains a hope of starting a new life in spite of Antony's death. If so, she may only be pretending to court death until Dolabella's admission of Caesar's plans makes her death a necessity.

These doubts and questions testify to the complexity and the contradictions inherent in the queen's character. There are depths to Cleopatra that we glimpse but to which we never gain total access.

She is beyond neat categories and tidy synopses. Indeed, as she prepares to make her final exit, she dons a role that, like her previous incarnations of hussy, enchantress, queen, and shrew, reflects only one aspect of her character. Ironically, she now strikes a pose as wife and nursing mother. As she applies the poison snakes to her skin, Cleopatra fulfills her desire to effect the quickest death in proper Roman fashion. In her quest to win a kind of Roman nobility worthy of Antony, she brags of becoming as constant as marble, her self no longer ruled by "the fleeting moon" (V.ii.236). But to understand Cleopatra in her final moments as a mere domestic, as an uncompromised lover and dutiful wife, is to reduce her to a single aspect of her character. She may claim to be as solid as marble, but before dying she reminds the audience (and herself) that she is made of something much less constant than stone: "I am fire and air; my other elements / I give to baser life" (V.ii.280–281).

SUMMARY & ANALYSIS

# Important Quotations Explained

1.          Let's grant it is not
    Amiss to tumble on the bed of Ptolemy,
    To give a kingdom for a mirth, to sit
    And keep the turn of tippling with a slave,
    To reel the streets at noon, and stand the buffet
    With knaves that smells of sweat. Say this becomes him—
    As his composure must be rare indeed
    Whom these things cannot blemish—yet must Antony
    No way excuse his foils when we do bear
    So great a weight in his lightness. If he filled
    His vacancy with his voluptuousness,
    Full surfeits and the dryness of his bones
    Call on him for't. But to confound such time
    That drums him from his sport, and speaks as loud
    As his own state and ours—'tis to be chid
    As we rate boys who, being mature in knowledge,
    Pawn their experience to the present pleasure,
    And so rebel to judgement.

                           (I.iv.16–33)

In Act I, scene iv, Caesar meets with Lepidus to discuss the threat that Pompey poses to the empire. Here, he chastises Antony for staying in Egypt, where he pursues pleasure at the expense of his duty to the state. Caesar's speech is significant for two reasons. First, it defines the Western sensibilities against which Cleopatra's Egypt is judged and by which Antony is ultimately measured. As Caesar dismisses Antony's passion for Cleopatra as boyish irresponsibility, he asserts the Roman expectation of duty over pleasure, reason over emotion. These competing worlds and worldviews provide the framework for understanding the coming clashes between Caesar and Antony, Antony and Cleopatra, and Cleopatra and Caesar.

    Second, Caesar's speech to Lepidus is significant for its suggestion that the oppositional worlds delineated here are a result of perception. For example, just as our perception of Antony changes according to the perceptions of other characters—to Caesar he is

49

negligent and mighty; to Cleopatra, noble and easily manipulated; to Enobarbus, worthy but misguided—so too our understanding of East and West depends upon the ways in which the characters perceive them. To Caesar, Alexandria is a den of iniquity where the noontime streets are filled with "knaves that smell of sweat." But we should resist his understanding as the essential definition of the East; we need only refer to Cleopatra's very similar description of a Roman street to realize that place, as much as character, in *Antony and Cleopatra*, is a quilt of competing perceptions: "[m]echanic slaves / With greasy aprons, rules, and hammers shall / Uplift us to the view" (V.ii.205–207).

2.    Upon her landing Antony sent to her,
      Invited her to supper. She replied
      It should be better he became her guest,
      Which she entreated. Our courteous Antony,
      Whom ne'er the word of 'No' woman heard speak,
      Being barbered ten times o'er, goes to the feast,
      And for his ordinary pays his heart
      For what his eyes eat only.
      . . .
                  I saw her once
      Hop forty paces through the public street,
      And having lost her breath, she spoke and panted,
      That she did make defect perfection,
      And breathless, pour forth breath.
      . . .
      Age cannot wither her, nor custom stale
      Her infinite variety. Other women cloy
      The appetites they feed, but she makes hungry
      Where most she satisfies. For vilest things
      Become themselves in her, that the holy priests
      Bless her when she is riggish.
                              (II.ii.225–245)

Enobarbus makes this speech, one of the most famous of the play. The lines before this oft-quoted passage begin with the description of Cleopatra floating down the Nile on her gilded barge. Enobarbus moves on to tell the men gathered on Pompey's ship how Antony met Cleopatra. It seems that the general, particularly susceptible to the wants of women, fell under the queen's spell immediately. Whatever power Antony had in relation to the queen, he surrenders it almost immediately—in fact, before the two even meet: "She replied / It should be better he became her guest," and Antony, never having denied a woman's wishes, agrees. In addition to demonstrating the queen's power over Antony, this passage describes Cleopatra's talent for performance. Her performance in "the public street" makes "defect"—her inability to breathe—"perfection." Whether sitting stately on her "burnished throne" (II.ii.197) or hopping "forty paces," Cleopatra never loses her ability to quicken the breath of her onlookers or persuade the "holy priests" to bless what they would certainly, in others, condemn.

3.      You take from me a great part of myself.
        Use me well in't. Sister, prove such a wife
        As my thoughts make thee, and as my farthest bond
        Shall pass on thy aproof. Most noble Antony,
        Let not the piece of virtue which is set
        Betwixt us as the cement of our love
        To keep it builded, be the ram to batter
        The fortress of it; for better might we
        Have loved without this mean if on both parts
        This be not cherished.

                                        (III.ii.24–33)

Following the advice that Agrippa offers him in Act II, scene ii, Caesar offers Antony his sister, Octavia, as a means of securing peace
between them. This gesture attests to the power that men ascribe to
women and female sexuality in this play. What men consider the
wrong kind of female sexuality—embodied proudly and openly by
Cleopatra—stands as a threat to men, their reason, and sense of
duty. What they consider the right kind, however, as represented by
the modest "piece of virtue" Octavia, promises to be "the cement"
of Caesar's love for Antony. Caesar's language, here, is particularly
important: the words he chooses to describe Antony's union to
Octavia and, by extension, his reunion with Caesar, belong to the
vocabulary of builders: "the *cement* of our love / To keep it *builded,*
be the ram to batter / The *fortress* of it" (emphasis added). This language makes an explicit connection between the private realm of
love and the public realm of the state, a connection that causes Caesar more than a little anxiety throughout the play.

QUOTATIONS

4.     Sometimes we see a cloud that's dragonish,
       A vapour sometime like a bear or lion,
       A towered citadel, a pendent rock,
       A forked mountain, or blue promontory
       With trees upon't that nod unto the world
       And mock our eyes with air. Thou hast seen these signs;
       They are black vesper's pageants.
       . . .
       That which is now a horse even with a thought
       The rack disdains, and makes it indistinct
       As water is in water.
       . . .
       Here I am Antony,
       Yet cannot hold this visible shape, my knave.
       I made these wars for Egypt, and the Queen—
       Whose heart I thought I had, for she had mine,
       Which whilst it was mine had annexed unto't
       A million more, now lost—she, Eros, has
       Packed cards with Caesar, and false-played my glory
       Unto an enemy's triumph.
       Nay, weep not, gentle Eros. There is left us
       Ourselves to end ourselves.

                                      (IV.xv.3–22)

After Cleopatra's ships abandon Antony in battle for the second time, the general faces the greatest defeat of his military career. Antony is accustomed only to victory, and his understanding of self leaves little room for defeat, either on the battlefield or in terms of love. As a Roman, Antony has a rigid perception of himself: he must live within the narrowly defined confines of the victor and hero or not live at all. Here, he complains to his trusted attendant, Eros, about the shifting of his identity. He feels himself helplessly changing, morphing from one man to another like a cloud that turns from a dragon to a bear to a lion as it moves across the sky. He tries desperately to cling to himself—"Here I am Antony"—but laments he "cannot hold this visible shape." Left without military might or Cleopatra, Antony loses his sense of who he is. Rather than amend his identity to incorporate this loss, rather than become an Antony conquered, he chooses to end his life. In the end, he clings to the image of himself as the unvanquished hero in order to achieve this last task: "[t]here is left us / Ourselves to end ourselves."

5.    Nay, 'tis most certain, Iras. Saucy lictors
       Will catch at us like strumpets, and scald rhymers
       Ballad us out o' tune. The quick comedians
       Extemporally will stage us, and present
       Our Alexandrian revels. Antony
       Shall be brought drunken forth, and I shall see
       Some squeaking Cleopatra boy my greatness
       I' th' posture of a whore.

                                  (V.ii.210–217)

Soon after Antony's death, Cleopatra determines to follow her lover into the afterlife. She commits to killing herself and, in Act V, scene ii, convinces her handmaids of the rightness of this decision. She conjures up a horrific image of the humiliation that awaits her as Caesar's trophy, employing the vocabulary of the theater, fearing that "quick comedians / Extemporally will stage us." She imagines that Antony will be played as a drunk, and a squeaking boy will portray her as a whore. Given that, throughout the play, Cleopatra is a consummate actress—we are never quite sure how much of her emotion is genuine and how much theatrical fireworks—her refusal to let either Antony or herself be portrayed in such a way is especially significant. To Cleopatra, the Roman understanding of her character and her relationship with Antony is a gross and unacceptable wrong. It does not mesh with the grandness of her self-perception—rather than being a queen of the order of Isis, she will go down in history "[i]' th' posture of a whore." Just as Antony cannot allow his self-image to expand to include defeat, Cleopatra refuses to allow her image to be stripped to its basest parts.

# KEY FACTS

FULL TITLE
*The Tragedy of Antony and Cleopatra*

AUTHOR
William Shakespeare

TYPE OF WORK
Play

GENRE
Tragedy

LANGUAGE
English

TIME AND PLACE WRITTEN
1606–1607, London, England

DATE OF FIRST PUBLICATION
Published in the First Folio of 1623

PUBLISHER
The First Folio was published by a group of printers, publishers, and booksellers: William and Isaac Jaggard, William Aspey, John Smethwick, and Edward Blount. Isaac Jaggard's and Edward Blount's names appear on the title page of the folio.

TONE
Tragic, poetic, grandiose, decadent, stoic

SETTING (TIME)
40–30 B.C.

SETTING (PLACE)
The Roman Empire and Egypt

PROTAGONIST
Mark Antony, one of the triumvirs of Rome

KEY FACTS

MAJOR CONFLICT

Antony is torn between his duties as a Roman ruler and soldier and his desire to live in Egypt with his lover, Cleopatra. This inner conflict leads him to become embroiled in a war with Caesar, one of his fellow triumvirs.

RISING ACTION

Caesar lures Antony out of Egypt and back to Rome, and marries Antony to his sister, Octavia. Antony eventually returns to Egypt and Cleopatra, and Caesar prepares to lead an army against Antony.

CLIMAX

Antony disgraces himself by fleeing the battle of Actium to follow Cleopatra, betraying his own image of himself as a noble Roman.

FALLING ACTION

Cleopatra abandons Antony during the second naval battle, leaving him to suffer an insurmountable defeat.

THEMES

The struggle between reason and emotion; the clash of East and West; the definition of honor

MOTIFS

Extravagant declarations of love; public displays of affection; female sexuality

SYMBOLS

Shape-changing clouds; Cleopatra's fleeing ships; the asps

FORESHADOWING

The play's repeated mentions of snakes—for instance, Lepidus's drunken ravings about the creatures of the Nile—foreshadow Cleopatra's chosen means of suicide.

KEY FACTS

# Study Questions & Essay Topics

## Study Questions

1.  *Discuss the structure of the play. How do the quick scene changes affect the plot?*

In sheer number of scenes, *Antony and Cleopatra* outstrips all other Shakespearean plays. Act V, scene ii, the longest scene in the play, is a mere 356 lines, a modest length compared to scenes in Shakespeare's other tragedies. The shortness of the scenes compresses our sense of both space and time. First, geographically speaking, the play shuttles the audience from one end of the Roman Empire to another, from Rome to Athens to Syria to Alexandria. The global span of the scenes mirrors the play's concern with the construction of an empire. Furthermore, the rapidly shifting scenes quicken the pace of the play and, with it, the audience's sense of the passage of time. Although *Antony and Cleopatra* covers a period of ten years, we feel that events follow one another immediately. For example, Ventidius's war against the Parthians takes no more time than Octavia's fateful journey from Athens to Rome. This compression of time speeds us toward the play's outcome, heightening the tragedy's sense of inevitability.

2.    *Contrast Cleopatra with Octavia. How is each
       representative of her civilization?*

Cleopatra and Octavia represent rival civilizations. Cleopatra's
beauty and seductiveness are without question. Even Enobarbus,
who resents the queen's command over Antony, acknowledges the
undeniable strength of her powers. In fact, his description of Cleopatra in Act II, scene ii offers the play's most complete picture of her
beauty and charms. In a world devoted to visual spectacles, Cleopatra's command over her physical appearance lends her a kind of
power that the plainer Octavia lacks. A single tear from Cleopatra
can turn Antony's anger into fawning devotion, whereas nothing
that Octavia does can bring him back from Alexandria. Octavia's
unheralded arrival in Rome symbolizes her near invisibility to her
husband. Described by Cleopatra's messenger as physically unimpressive, Octavia possesses a temperament that, when compared to
the queen's, is equally unimpressive. When betrayed by Antony,
Octavia summons none of the rage or indignation or sorrow that
one could easily imagine might come from Cleopatra. In her ability
to shift from one extreme emotion to another, the queen embodies
the unfettered passions that Caesar and the other disciplined
Romans view as a threat to their Western order. Octavia, who in
contrast seems rather passionless—after all, Antony's abandon-
ment brings only the meekest tears—represents an easily contained
and easily controlled type of female sexuality that does not threaten
men's reason or rule. Thus, she becomes, as Maecenas notes, the
"love and pity" of every Roman heart (III.vi.92).

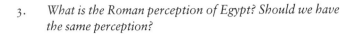

3.   *What is the Roman perception of Egypt? Should we have
     the same perception?*

Among the Romans in the play, there is a definite consensus regarding Egypt. Philo sets the tone for the West's perception of the East in the opening lines of the play, when he complains that Antony, the paragon of Western military might and discipline, has been led to distraction by "a gipsy's lust" (I.i.10). Caesar seconds Philo's opinion when he condemns Antony for abandoning his "kingdom for a mirth" (I.iv.18). According to the Romans, who pride themselves on the strength of their reason as much as the strength of their army, Egypt is a land in which emotions overshadow rationality, passions dominate and derail the intellect, and pleasure takes priority over duty. Even Antony, whose love for Cleopatra makes him much more sympathetic than his comrades to Egyptian culture, considers Egypt a threat to his identity as a Roman: "These strong Egyptian fetters I must break, / Or lose myself in dotage" (I.ii.105–106).

We should not share this perception of Egypt, however. For the Roman understanding of the East and, by extension, its representative queen is exceptionally narrow. According to Caesar, for instance, Cleopatra is little more than the whore for whom Antony has sacrificed his kingdom and reputation. But just as Cleopatra is a multidimensional character who plays the parts of lovesick devotee, grief-stricken mourner, jealous harpy, and even, at the end, wife and mother as convincingly as she dons the role of seductress, so too the East contains more than simple base temptations. A homeland of sorts for the passions, freedoms, and imagination that often escape the likes of Caesar and Antony, Shakespeare's East is best understood as a world larger and more complex than reductive Roman thought allows.

QUESTIONS & ESSAYS

# SUGGESTED ESSAY TOPICS

1.  Discuss Enobarbus's relationship with Antony. Is his defection justified?

2.  Analyze Antony's decline. Do his mistakes make him cease to be heroic?

3.  Analyze Antony and Cleopatra's relationship, paying close attention to their trust in one another.

4.  Compare and contrast Cleopatra with Caesar, especially in their final confrontation.

5.  Shakespearean tragic heroes tend to die cleanly and grandly when they take their own lives. Antony, on the other hand, botches his suicide. Why is this detail significant? What does it suggest about his character or the play?

6.  Contrast the characters of Octavius Caesar and Mark Antony. What qualities allow Caesar to win their war?

# Review & Resources

## Quiz

1. In the play's opening scene, why do the Roman soldiers fault Antony?

   A. He is overly ambitious and plans to divide the Roman state by waging war against Caesar

   B. His cowardice in battle has resulted in the loss of valuable sea trade routes to Pompey

   C. His excessive fondness for Cleopatra threatens to compromise his duties as a Roman statesman

   D. An irresponsible drinker, Antony often treats his subordinates disrespectfully

2. What do Charmian and Iras do in order to foresee their futures?

   A. Consult a crystal ball

   B. Summon a soothsayer, who reads their palms

   C. Read tea leaves

   D. Visit a witch

3. How does Antony react to the news of Fulvia's death?

   A. He regrets having wished her dead and wishes her back

   B. He weeps uncontrollably

   C. He chastises Cleopatra for keeping him from his true family

   D. The news does not faze him

4.   Why does Caesar condemn Antony for abandoning Rome?

    A.   He does not like the fact that Antony is having more fun than he is

    B.   He cannot collect taxes on Antony's unoccupied lands

    C.   He himself loves Cleopatra and is jealous of Antony's relationship with her

    D.   He and Lepidus are left with the unfair burden of responding to Pompey's armies by themselves

5.   Upon leaving Egypt, what does Antony send to Cleopatra as a gift?

    A.   A golden comb

    B.   A pearl

    C.   A snake-shaped bracelet

    D.   A cask of fine wine

6.   What solution does Agrippa propose to establish peace between Caesar and Antony?

    A.   Antony should make a public apology for neglecting his duties to the empire

    B.   Antony should marry Caesar's sister, Octavia

    C.   Antony should turn over a portion of his kingdom to Caesar

    D.   Both men should drink heartily and forget the past

7.   Why, according to the Soothsayer, should Antony leave Rome?

    A.   As long as Antony remains in Rome, his fortune will be overshadowed by Caesar's

    B.   Caesar is plotting with Octavia to take Antony's life

    C.   Cleopatra will make life miserable for him unless he returns to her

    D.   Antony's new devotion to pleasure has compromised his military might, and he would surely be defeated in a battle with Pompey

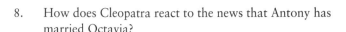

8.  How does Cleopatra react to the news that Antony has married Octavia?

    A.  She faints
    B.  She sends Antony a letter demanding that he never return to Egypt
    C.  She beats her messenger, then orders him to go and size up the competition
    D.  She courts Caesar in hopes that he will destroy Antony

9.  The triumvirs offer Pompey control of Sicily and Sardinia in exchange for what?

    A.  His word that he will not attack any of the empire's lands or interests
    B.  Ridding the seas of pirates and furnishing Rome with supplies of wheat
    C.  Welcoming Antony's mother on her upcoming visit to Sicily
    D.  A percentage of the goods seized by his navy

10. How does Pompey react to Menas's suggestion that they kill the Roman triumvirs and thereby make Pompey the most powerful man alive?

    A.  He appreciates the thought but urges Menas to await a more fitting time to attack the triumvirs
    B.  He is dismayed by Menas's disregard for human life
    C.  He tells Menas to do whatever needs to be done to secure him control of the world
    D.  He wishes Menas had done the deed without telling him

11.  Why does Ventidius refuse to push on into Parthia?

    A.    Without Antony's leadership, he fears defeat

    B.    Like Caesar, his soldiers resent Antony's loyalty to Egypt and cannot be counted on to fight further battles in Antony's name

    C.    He has lost too many soldiers and does not want to lose more

    D.    He does not want to win Antony's disfavor by outperforming him in battle

12.  When Cleopatra's messenger brings word to his queen that Antony has married Octavia, she beats him severely. Later, though, she praises this same man for his good service. What brings about this change of heart?

    A.    The messenger reports that Octavia is plain-looking and generally unimpressive

    B.    Charmian convinces Cleopatra that it is morally reprehensible to abuse one's servants

    C.    Fickle as she is, Cleopatra merely forgets the news of Antony's marriage

    D.    Cleopatra's recent conversion to Christianity

13.  After arriving in Athens, why does Antony send Octavia immediately back to Rome?

    A.    He cannot pretend that he loves her as he loves Cleopatra

    B.    He wishes her to make peace between himself and Caesar, who has disparaged his name in public

    C.    Due to political strife in Greece, he fears that Octavia is not safe there

    D.    He cannot stand Octavia's bickering

14.  What does Cleopatra contribute to Antony's battle with Caesar?

    A.    A fleet of sixty ships

    B.    An army of ten thousand soldiers

    C.    An amulet to protect Antony in battle

    D.    A golden dagger

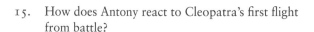

15. How does Antony react to Cleopatra's first flight
from battle?

   A.  He thanks the gods, for battle is no place for a woman
   B.  He follows her and leads his troops in a retreat
   C.  He praises her assessment of the situation
   D.  He admits to Enobarbus that she is an unworthy
       object of affection

16. How does Cleopatra repay Antony after leading him
into a retreat?

   A.  With a kiss
   B.  With the promise of marriage
   C.  By giving him her kingdom
   D.  By agreeing to seduce Caesar so that Antony may
       kill him

17. What does Antony request of Caesar after losing the battle
to him?

   A.  To be publicly vilified for his cowardly behavior
   B.  To be judged fairly by a jury of his peers
   C.  To be allowed to live in Egypt with Cleopatra
   D.  To be allowed to return to Rome and resume his
       marriage to Octavia

18. How does Antony react to the news of Caesar's refusal to
grant him permission to live in Egypt?

   A.  He becomes enraged and determines to challenge
       Caesar in one-on-one combat
   B.  He fakes his own death in hopes of living with
       Cleopatra in secrecy
   C.  He travels to Parthia in hopes of mounting another
       army against his enemy
   D.  He surrenders himself to Caesar's soldiers

REVIEW & RESOURCES

19. On the night before his fight with Caesar, what sign of bad
fortune do Antony's soldiers encounter?

    A.    A full moon
    B.    A black cat
    C.    Strange music
    D.    A man with no legs

20. How does Antony react to the news of
Enobarbus's desertion?

    A.    He curses his friend's disloyalty
    B.    He vows to kill Enobarbus after he kills Caesar
    C.    He believes that every man must follow his
            own conscience and therefore respects
            Enobarbus's decision
    D.    He grieves for having corrupted an honest man and
            orders his friend's possessions returned to him

21. How does Enobarbus react to Antony's gift
and well-wishes?

    A.    He feels extreme guilt and determines to die rather
            than fight him
    B.    He believes that Antony has lost his mind, which only
            validates Enobarbus's decision to abandon him
    C.    He realizes he has made a terrible mistake and rushes
            back to Antony to beg his forgiveness
    D.    He gives the treasure to the peasants of Alexandria
            and goes off to live in the desert

22. What does Charmian suggest that Cleopatra do in order to
quell Antony's anger against her?

    A.    Publicly denounce Caesar
    B.    Send him word that she has killed herself
    C.    Write him a love letter
    D.    Leave Alexandria

23. Whom does Antony order to kill him?

    A. Enobarbus
    B. Mardian
    C. Diomedes
    D. Eros

24. What does Caesar intend to do with Cleopatra after Antony's death?

    A. Marry her
    B. Keep her on display in Rome
    C. Kill her
    D. Send her into exile

25. How does Cleopatra kill herself?

    A. She stabs herself with a dagger
    B. She jumps from the top of her monument
    C. She lets herself be bitten by poisonous snakes
    D. She drowns herself in the Nile

ANSWER KEY:
1: C; 2: B; 3: A; 4: D; 5: B; 6: B; 7: A; 8: C; 9: B; 10: D;
11: D; 12: A; 13: B; 14: A; 15: B; 16: A; 17: C; 18: A; 19: C;
20: D; 21: A; 22: B; 23: D; 24: B; 25: C

## Suggestions for Further Reading

BARROLL, J. LEEDS. *Shakespearean Tragedy: Genre, Tradition, and Change in* ANTONY AND CLEOPATRA. Washington, D.C.: Folger Books, 1984.

BLOOM, HAROLD. *Shakespeare: The Invention of the Human.* New York: Riverhead Books, 1998.

BROWN, JOHN RUSSELL. ANTONY AND CLEOPATRA: *A Casebook.* Basingstoke: Macmillan Education, 1991.

GRANVILLE-BARKER, HARLEY. *Prefaces to Shakespeare.* Princeton, New Jersey: Princeton University Press, 1946.

HEILMAN, ROBERT, ed. *Shakespeare: The Tragedies.* Englewood Cliffs, New Jersey: Prentice-Hall, 1984.

MILES, GEOFFREY. *Shakespeare and the Constant Romans.* New York: Clarendon Press, 1996.

ROSE, MARK, ed. *Twentieth Century Interpretations of* ANTONY AND CLEOPATRA: *A Collection of Critical Essays.* Englewood Cliffs, New Jersey: Prentice-Hall, 1977.

SCHANZER, ERNEST. *The Problem Plays of Shakespeare: A Study of* JULIUS CAESAR, MEASURE FOR MEASURE, *and* ANTONY AND CLEOPATRA. New York: Schocken Books, 1963.

THOMAS, VIVIAN. *Shakespeare's Roman Worlds.* New York: Routledge, 1989.

WOFFORD, SUSANNE L., ed. *Shakespeare's Late Tragedies: A Collection of Critical Essays.* Upper Saddle River, New Jersey: Prentice-Hall, 1996.

## A Note on the Type

The typeface used in SparkNotes study guides is Sabon, created by master typographer Jan Tschichold in 1964. Tschichold revolutionized the field of graphic design twice: first with his use of asymmetrical layouts and sanserif type in the 1930s when he was affiliated with the Bauhaus, then by abandoning assymetry and calling for a return to the classic ideals of design. Sabon, his only extant typeface, is emblematic of his latter program: Tschichold's design is a recreation of the types made by Claude Garamond, the great French typographer of the Renaissance, and his contemporary Robert Granjon. Fittingly, it is named for Garamond's apprentice, Jacques Sabon.

# SPARKNOTES
# TEST PREPARATION
# GUIDES

The SparkNotes team figured it was time to cut standardized tests down to size. We've studied the tests for you, so that SparkNotes test prep guides are:

## *Smarter:*
Packed with critical-thinking skills and test-
taking strategies that will improve your score.

## *Better:*
Fully up to date, covering all new features of the tests,
with study tips on every type of question.

## *Faster:*
Our books cover exactly what you need to
know for the test. No more, no less.

SAT and PSAT are registered trademarks of the College Entrance Examination Board, which does not endorse these books.
ACT is a registered trademark of ACT, Inc. which neither sponsors nor endorses these books.

# SparkNotes Study Guides: